For Better or For Worse
The 10th Anniversary Collection

A Look Inside...

For Better or For Worse

The 10th Anniversary Collection

By Lynn Johnston

Andrews and McMeel

A Universal Press Syndicate Company

Kansas City · New York

Library of Congress Catalog Card Number: 89–84811

ISBN: 0-8362-1853-1

Text design by Rick Cusick

Cover photo by Dave Palangio

The cartoons appearing on pages 48–53 are taken from *David, We're
Pregnant,* copyright © 1975 by Lynn Johnston, *Hi Mom! Hi Dad!,* copyright
© 1977 by Lynn Johnston, and *Do They Ever Grow Up,* copyright © 1978 by
Lynn Johnston, reprinted by permission of Meadowbrook Press, 18318
Minnetonka Blvd., Deephaven, Minnesota.

First Printing, September 1989
Third Printing, March 1993

For Len Norris

whose wonderful comic

illustrations made me

want to draw.

Contents

Acknowledgments

When I began to write "a little bit about myself" for this book, I never thought I would write so much.

After every epic, there is always a list of credits, and I must give credit where it is due.

I thank my parents for the gifts of words and wit, art and music, and for the stable home we grew up in. I thank my husband for being strong enough and secure enough to live with my obsessions and me! I thank my children for allowing themselves to be identified with Michael and Elizabeth and the fictitious lives they lead.

Thanks also to the teachers and other cartoonists who have influenced, advised, and befriended me over the years. I must also remember Jim Andrews who saw potential in my work and sent me a contract ten years ago! Thanks, Jim. It's been a wonderful ten years!

For Better or For Worse
The 10th Anniversary Collection

MISS MURIEL STEWART said I was the only kid she'd ever expelled from kindergarten. Having been chastised already for taking off all my clothes during a game of hide-and-seek (I wanted to make being found more interesting), I had broken the light bulb that hung from a cord in the front hall.

Risking another stint in her broom closet with a mouthful of soap, I had stood contemplating that light bulb. Let the others march in circles to some inane melody; a challenge was a challenge. It was a long hall with a high ceiling made darker still by the wallpaper, a somber repetitive pattern of magenta nosegays and brown wreaths. The bulb hung there, naked; vulnerable. If I stood on the telephone chair, I knew I could reach it with a yardstick, making the shadows in the hall rise and fall as the light swung. The first attempt was successful. I imagined I was a prisoner in the hold of some great ship. Living across the street had given me the moxie that comes with being on familiar territory. I smacked the bulb again . . . too hard.

With the offending yardstick still in my hand, Miss Stewart propelled me by my right ear down her path, through the iron gate, and across 5th Street which had not yet been paved. Tar and gravel stuck to my feet which barely touched the ground as I tried to keep up with her brisk, angry stride.

Our small blue and white frame was kept spotless inside and out. The sheers were gone from the front windows, so I knew that my mother was doing one of her spring cleaning extravaganzas.

Miss Stewart released my ear and deposited me on the front porch. She made an authoritative rap on the door, opened it, and pushed me inside. Miss Stewart was a short gray-haired woman of about fifty. Generally her manner was pleasant and unassuming. Today, she was a picture from Grimm's.

"I have had it, Mrs. Ridgway!" she began. "You can plead and reason with me, but I've made up my mind. I cannot cope with this child any longer." My mother looked up from the spot on the hardwood floor where she was kneeling. This had come as no surprise to her. She wiped the moist hair from her brow, and sighed, "I wish this could have waited till the floors dried."

I wanted to make hide-and-seek more interesting.

Kindergarten had been a chore: an endless parade of colored shapes, nursery songs, and playtime bands in which I always got the triangle. The dumb triangle! Everyone else got drums or flutes or, best of all, the one tambourine—but I always got the triangle. No matter how hard you hit it, the result was always a barely audible "ping" and it became the symbol of all I hated about kindergarten.

It was a relief to be free of Miss Stewart's somber brown house, the white pressed-board studio, the kids who always seemed to do the right thing, and her cats.

Everyone in the world seemed to have a best friend those days but me. These were times when your best friend was your companion exclusively. You became blood brothers (spit was easier), you swore on the Bible, you pledged allegiance forever, you became one. To accompany a different kid to the corner store for gumballs and Coke was paramount to infidelity. I wanted to have a friend like that.

There was no question that I was loved at home. Ours was a house full of music and chatter and neighbors dropping in for tea, but as Elizabeth said in one of the strips, "I know you like me, Dad—but I want *real* friends." I felt I had to get out there and win 'em over any way that I could. My methods were rarely appropriate. No noise was too vulgar, no prank too risky, no rule went untested—and if I got a laugh, then the inevitable punishment was worthwhile.

Being sent home from the neighborhood kindergarten was a sort of freedom for all of us. In my room was a fantasy world of my own making into which I seemed to fit more easily than I did into the real world outside. In my room, which I shared with my younger brother, were toys and books and junk—but my real escape was paper. I hoarded it. I kept old greeting cards, box tops, notepaper—anything I could draw on, and in a state of wakeful dreaming, I would see images appear, my imagination come to life, my right hand drawing my thoughts on paper. Even to me, the gift was magic.

Whenever I'm near a schoolyard or in a classroom, I look for the little kid who was me. Now and then, I find the troublemaker, the clown, the extrovert—just slightly out of control.

I always got the triangle.

As our eyes meet, we smile in mutual recognition, for we know all too well that the silliness is a mask for what's really going on inside. Only experience and time help to channel this behavior, and although I'm grateful for the onset of maturity, I'm grateful too for the memory that propels me back in time.

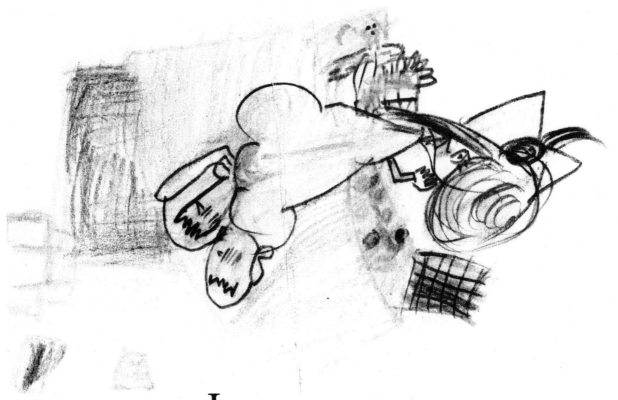

A drawing I did around the age of 4.

I remember grade one. I remember the room, the windows, Myrna who sat in front of me, Ruby, the first kid in school to get glasses, Jean who was Native Indian and never looked up when she smiled, the feel of new erasers, the taste of library paste—grade one was everything that kindergarten was not. Here was a challenge!

I could already read. My mother was a calligrapher and I watched for hours as she inscribed with india ink on the fine cream-colored paper that my granddad bought. Page after page of his stamp collections bore the careful ruling and artistry of my mother's pen, and I learned to love the characters she drew even before I recognized them as the alphabet. Reading gave me confidence. Reading gave me status, and although my continuing raucous behavior never seemed to win friends, I certainly influenced people.

Richard Taylor sat next to me, second to last row, grade one, North Vancouver Elementary School. Richard was an affable kid with a perpetually runny nose, and not too bright. Like myself, he'd do anything to amuse, and it was his glorious gullibility that appealed to me the most. If I told him to yell, he would. If I told him to fire a spitball, he would. Richard was my kind of guy.

At the back of the class was the cloakroom: a long, narrow closet lined with coat hooks, a shelf for lunch pails, and under each coat, in neat, orderly pairs, were the omnipresent rubber boots. Rubber boots were part of a west coast kid's anatomy. They came in black or olive green. If your socks weren't long enough, they'd wear the skin off the backs of your legs, making a rough, stinging smile. I hated them.

The most consistent punishment doled out to grade one offenders was a five-minute stint in the cloakroom. I was in there often, contemplating the array of outerwear, wishing I had a genuine Maggie Muggins lunch pail and matching thermos like Carol Falconer's. I would stand there, thinking . . . and I'd eye that long line of rubber boots.

"Richard," I whispered, "fall out of your seat." It had been a particularly uneventful morning and subtraction was beginning to bore. Richard eagerly obliged. A pleasurable round of muffled snorts and giggles ensued. "The cloakroom, Richard!" Mrs. Hindmarch announced predictably—"now." Richard rose and dutifully turned to follow orders. "Richard!" I whispered again as he shuffled past my desk. "Pee in the rubber boots!"

Richard's aim and bladder capacity were admirable. It was lunchtime before we discovered that he had indeed peed in the rubber boots. Every one of them. Even mine.

Accepting partial responsibility for the event was the easy part. Bad P.R. was, after all, better than no attention at all. But, washing out all those boots with the school garden hose made me wonder if it was all worthwhile. Somehow, deep inside, I knew it was.

Dated December 1951—at the age of 4½

Ask any cartoonist—especially the ones who draw kids and chaos—and they'll tell you they remember their childhood in minute detail. Ask them where they get their ideas. Ten to one the answer will be "Who knows?" But, in truth, they come from the research into every obscure corner of that youthful and innocent past. With the recall of every injustice, every fear, every act of courage, each schoolyard stone that's overturned gives rise to inspiration. It's all part of the "gift."

"For Better or For Worse" has allowed me to dig as far back

Drawings done between 7 and 8 years old.

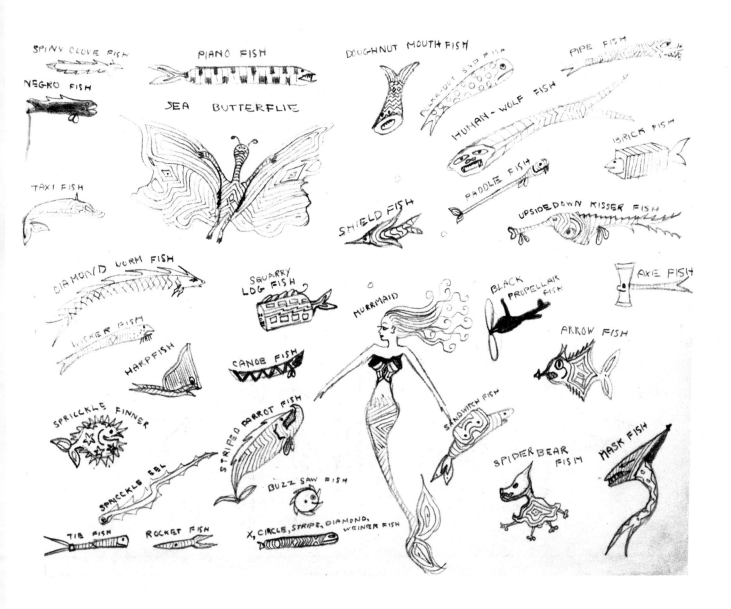

I remember drawing this one in fifth grade.

into my past as I care to go. To give life to even an imaginary character is to become that character and I have become each of the four people I try so candidly to describe. Sure, I take everyday situations and twist them or embellish them, but the emotions, the essence of the kids especially, come from my need to dwell on the past.

Elizabeth is me at the age of two melting crayons on the radiator; Michael is me at the age of six feeling jealousy and rage at the coddling of a younger sibling. Every fight, every faux pas I send to the paper, is an admission of personal guilt and the publication of them is as cleansing as the classified ad that reads, "Thanks to the blessed St. Jude for favors received." To admit one's shortcomings is to, perhaps, be absolved.

I was three and my brother Alan barely six months old when we moved from Collingwood, Ontario, to British Columbia. Dad was a jeweler and a watchmaker and, hoping to find work in Vancouver, he moved the family west.

A family photo taken in my grandfather's garden when I was 10.

At age 4 with my brother Alan, age 2

For a few months, we lived with my grandparents in their dark, Tudor house overlooking the sea. My mother had been trained as Granddad's private secretary before she left home for England during the war, and did the painstaking illustrations and calligraphy that made some of his customers' stamp collections among the most beautiful and valuable in the country. Ursula Bainbridge and Merv Ridgway both enlisted in the Royal Canadian Air Force and met, overseas, on an air force base in the town of Linton-on-Ouze, England. When the squadrons returned home, they were married and settled in Collingwood, Ontario. Dad had grown up there, but with business prospects dim and a wife who longed for the west coast, he pulled up his roots, and now, with two toddlers in tow, started again, this time on my mother's home turf. While Dad took the ferry into the city every day, my mother continued to work for her father who, by the time I was five had become one of Canada's foremost stamp dealers and experts on the art of forgery.

More fascinating for me than the stamps themselves were the heavy, smooth-surfaced cards they were mounted on. My mother would draw fine lines around each stamp, framing them like miniature paintings, and when these pages were revised, the old ones were discarded. These treasures came to me.

From as early as I can recall I drew tiny pictures in boxes, row on row, bringing thoughts and fantasies to life.

I drew these at the age of 11.

I inherited my mother's ability to draw, and from my father, I inherited the love of silliness. Music and a good laugh are the things he lives for. He was born to entertain, to storytell. I don't believe he's forgotten a joke he's ever heard. In fact, despite my mother's rather Victorian upbringing, she too had a gift for puns and wordplay.

If my parents did not communicate with the openness and directness one expects today, they communicated with humor. If you can't say it right out . . . joke about it.

Two years apart in age, high-strung, and constantly seeking attention, Alan and I were always at each other's throats. Though there was little money for extras, we were both encouraged to expand our interests (beyond the need to witness the other's demise). Alan took trumpet lessons, beginning his career as a performer; I was enrolled in every Saturday morning art class the community had available, setting a path for me. We were artistic rivals and it's unfortunate that we spent more time trying to do each other in than in pooling our natural resources. On rare occasions we would come together in mutual, wonderfully satisfying mischief. What havoc we could have wrung, had we been in synch!

Downstairs, in the basement, Dad had a workbench on which lay a confusing jumble of miniature screwdrivers, tweezers, wheels, containers, and odd machinery. He made $47 a week working at Shores Jewelers in the city. He made extra cash at home repairing rings, clocks, and watches—and even an occasional music box came in.

His talent for making things go was matched by his great generosity. "Give me a sweet smile," he would often say to a child or a woman coming in for a repair. His unwillingness to charge a friend for his labor was both endearing and frustrating for, in truth, we needed every cent he could make down there.

That bench was a constant source of interest. "Look but don't touch," Dad would say, his face contorted to one side, his cheek and brushy eyebrow holding the glass to his eye.

It was a Saturday morning and Alan and I had been left at home alone. At the age of eight or nine, it was not unusual for me to be left to supervise as Mom walked down to the shops. She was never gone long.

Boredom having set in (there was no TV—we didn't get one of those until I was twelve!) we wandered down into the basement, an unfinished catacomb of naked studs, laundry appliances, spider webs, and . . . the workbench.

On the forbidden workbench was the biggest old clock we had ever seen. It was a chime clock. The face and hands lay expressionless, side by side. The great wooden case sat like a carcass; the guts removed. The intricate brass-colored workings were fascinating. The gears and wheels were in place, the great mainspring was coiled and ready. The key was there.

Alan put the key in place and turned. The wheels moved with slow, rhythmic precision. Each gear passed the other, fitting one into the next like fine chewing teeth. "I bet," he mused, "that if we ran some paper through those wheels, they'd make holes in it!" He was right. We fed one sheet of paper through the workings of the clock, then another. *"Tickets!"* Alan cried, as the perforations made long even rows—and, tickets we made.

Once we had tickets, we needed a show. Behind the furnace were the laundry lines used on rainy days. These were also used for Mother's very personal stuff. Every wash day, the family laundry was hung in a perfect line outside—minus Mother's underwear. Bras, corsets, garter belts, slips, and panties were always hung in the privacy of the basement.

It was to view this intimate, personal collection that we sold the tickets.

It wasn't the worst thing we'd ever done. Boiling eggs till they ran dry to see if they'd explode took precedence over this. (Eggs do, indeed, explode.) But it was far from the most popular.

The tickets were a dime apiece and included a refreshment of Ritz crackers and Kool-Aid, following the "show." We made a sum total of sixty cents.

Mother was furious. The injustice done in permitting the neighborhood kids to view her intimate apparel was more than she could bear.

When Father came home, the case was presented and there was no opportunity for defense. The four of us trooped into the basement to review this most heinous of crimes.

The clock, though somewhat in need of cleaning, was still in working order. Dad examined it and fingered the remaining tickets.

With indignant expression and short-clipped speech, Mother laid her case. "This," she concluded, "was a blatant disregard for my personal privacy!"

Alan and I hung our heads, ready for Dad to pronounce sentence upon us. No words came from the head of the household. "Well?" Mother prodded.

"But, Ursie," he stammered, holding the confiscated sixty cents in his outstretched palm. "This is the most money I've made off that bench all week!"

If Mom was the authoritarian, Dad was often our ally. Those two unwittingly played off each other like straight man and comic, and not a little of it rubbed off on us.

Fifth Street was sort of a middle of the road living; not near enough to the shipyards to be called lower class, and not close enough to St. Andrews Church to be considered well off, either.

When Luccia Messina moved onto our street, my search for a best friend was over. Lucy, who could barely speak English, communicated with her hands and her expressions; her exuberance and laughter were infectious. We became inseparable.

Unlike my own rather conservative household, hers was a raucous place full of shouting and noise and kitchen clatter. This was a family of few inhibitions, and Lucy was game for anything.

Together we hunted rotten eggs in the bush near the Doucette's chicken coop, played marbles, made whistles out of grass, and made a ceremony of going to the Odeon Theatre's Saturday afternoon matinee.

Again, I have to thank my father for sharpening our interest in comedy. Who else would show you just how to trip on a rug, how to artfully tell a joke, how to get the most out of a pair of loose pants?

Alan, Luccia, and I took in every Abbott and Costello, every

The house on 5th Street was my home for 20 years.

Charlie Chaplin, every Three Stooges film the industry could supply. No pratfall or sight gag was too difficult to stage. Today, these films are still the most outstanding examples of the intricate and illusive art of comedy.

It was Dad who honed our interest in theater, but it was Granddad's serious analysis of the newspaper comic strips that, for me, brought these two dimensional comedies to life.

I was an artist. There was no question about it. I was going to be an artist like my Aunt Unity. Everyone said so and I knew it was true. I had been able to draw since the age of two. I accepted it.

Although my mother's eldest sister was a gifted and prolific painter, Granddad had little use for "art" as a career, and made no secret of his disdain for her profession. In fact, Granddad did not seem to have much use for women altogether, and I often felt a great disparity in his treatment of my brother and me.

The only time a closeness was permitted between us was when he read the comics. He took them seriously. These were not merely vacuous fillers of space, but bright, social commentary, and he had an opinion reserved for each one of them.

Pogo was his ultimate favorite. Walt Kelly, he revered as the preeminent observer of man and his politics; a poet ahead of his time. Although I never really understood *Pogo,* I was impressed by Kelly's ability to draw. His expressions were perfect, and his lines rich with movement.

Granddad pontificated on the vulgarity of the Katzenjammers, the gluttony of Dagwood, the plight of Orphan Annie. He cut out and kept entire series of *Lil' Abner,* he knew every Dick Tracy plot—but, when it came to *Peanuts,* he was stumped. "Children don't have thoughts like that!" he'd bluster, as Charlie Brown would offer a fitting retort to Lucy's caustic psychiatrist. "Children don't have the ability to understand adult situations! They don't have that sort of sophistication!"

Until *Peanuts* appeared, I tended to agree with all of my grandfather's pronouncements, but about this one strip, he was dead wrong. No other strip, except for perhaps *Miss Peach,* featured children as intuitive, articulate people, with all the thoughts and responses and abilities we knew we had! *Peanuts* not only made kids worth listening to, it featured women as strong, dominant characters. Women were equals. This new strip was as refreshing to us as it was to the free-spirited adults who embraced its honesty

Figures influenced by Barbie dolls.

with open arms. *Peanuts* became my favorite, and although my work differs in many ways, it is surely the model on which I've based my style of writing and timing.

If I enjoyed the Saturday funnies, then I was addicted to *Little Lulu.* I waited for each new issue, and gladly parted with the ten cents it cost to experience yet another adventure with Tubby and Witch Hazel and the rest. The stories and pictures came alive for me. I never laughed so hard as I did when Tubby ate a raw potato because it looked exactly like him! The repetition of "munch, munch, munch, munch, munch, . . . GULP!" and the facial expressions had me literally on the floor. I wanted to be able to make someone laugh like that. I wanted to be able to draw like that.

I also loved the Scrooge McDuck Stories—a bottomless vault of money truly struck my fancy. Scrooge was my grandfather in comic relief. Granddad was considered, by us, to be incredibly wealthy—but miserly beyond belief. When I laughed at Scrooge, I laughed at him.

Comic books in general were a real *need* for me; a key to survival in what I perceived to be a lonely world. When my mother made us give up comic books for Lent, it was the longest penance I'd ever done!

One of the first captioned drawings I did, age 11.

Even though Luccia Messina was my first real girlfriend, as we entered the higher grades in school, others entered our circle.

Elly Jansen was a shy, quiet girl. She was Dutch, and her mother often dressed her in gingham dresses and put large, white bows in her hair. Though our temperaments were worlds apart, we shared much in common. And by the end of the first quarter of seventh grade, we were close and loyal friends.

Elly and I would bike-ride together, we were home economics partners, we spent many weekends together, and I cared for her as deeply and honestly as one person could care for another.

I was still a rowdy, clowning, impulsive kid, whose behavior, more often than not, got me into trouble. She was my stable, studious complement, and together, we made perfect harmony.

Elly was beautiful. I was overweight, freckled, and mouse-haired; I considered myself cloddish and ugly next to her. Her delicate features and long, walnut-colored hair made her look like a porcelain doll. Elly was extraordinary.

Both of us were from strong, religious families; hers Catholic, mine Anglican. With an unquestioning faith, we believed in God, and as children, we thought we would live forever.

I remember Elly's headaches. She would come with Luccia and me to the movies, and she would close her eyes when the pain was too strong. She rarely complained, although we could see she was in agony. It dulled her eyes and made her shrink from the light and the sounds around us. We never knew how ill she really was.

It was Christmas. We were all home for the holidays. Elly walked up to her mother in the kitchen, and collapsed on the floor. She was taken to the hospital, where they tried to remove a large tumor from her head, but she died on the operating table.

Returning to school after Christmas break was hard for us all. Elly had been a favorite. Looking at her empty seat was gut-wrenching, agonizing, the ache went to the center of my heart and stayed there.

Mr. Lowney tried to explain to us that this was life, that we were to be grateful for having had her as our friend for even a short time. He told us that she was in heaven and would be with us always, and then he broke down and cried. Lucy was the first to run up to him. I was next. One by one the entire class of seventh grade students came to the front of the room. We threw our arms around each other and formed a solid wall around him, comforting him, comforting ourselves. It was a day of intense emotion and it made a family out of our one small class.

When Elly died, I lost my faith in God. I was a teenager with a mind of my own, and despite all of the religious outpourings and biblical rationale, it was gone. I left my position in the church choir. I stopped going to services altogether, and although I professed to have abandoned my faith, I wrote long heart-felt letters to her and burned them, hoping she'd read the phantom thoughts and forgive me for not knowing how seriously ill she was; for not being there when she died. You do strange things when you're grieving.

Years later, I sat signing books in a shop in North Vancouver. It was my sixth *For Better or For Worse* collection and I was on tour. An attractive, dark-haired woman came up to the table and put her hand on mine. "Do you remember me?" she asked. I put down my pen, stood up, and threw my arms around Luccia's neck. "You see? You see? I *do* know her," she said to her two very pretty teenaged daughters. She looked no different to me, though we hadn't seen each other in over twenty years. We laughed and clasped hands and said the usual things about home and family but when the introductions were over, we both wanted to ask the same thing. "Lynn," she whispered aside, "do you remember Elly?" The flood of emotions on that day came back to both of us as we stood there years later, as mothers of children Elly's age. Indeed, some things stay with you forever.

Sometime during my prepubescence, I discovered *Mad* magazine and looked forward to furtive exchanges with kids whose mothers did not disapprove of this radical and "absolutely dreadful" new publication. The more my mother condemned it, the better I liked it. I had begun to actively study comic drawing and names like Drucker and Jaffee and Martin were spoken with as much reverence by my crowd as the names of famed sports heroes were bounced around by the jocks. The writers and cartoonists of *Mad* were akin to genius. While others aspired to invent antigravity devices or qualify for the Olympics, my cronies yearned to be part of the magic circle that produced this great, sarcastic wit.

By the time I'd entered high school, my drawing style was beginning to jell. I still copied from heroes—especially Len Norris of the *Vancouver Sun*—but I could see that, slowly, my own "signature" was forming. When someone saw a particular kind of drawing, they knew it was mine! I'd learned how to control my temper and the silliness was almost in check. I actually worked hard at the subjects I liked, I became editor of the annual, and learned how to play the guitar. I was part of an improv theatre group who did terrible Goon Show imitations and wrote poetry on the injustices of life. This was the beginning of the sixties and I was as much an advocate of peace, love, and nonviolent protest as everyone else. I was attending the Vancouver School of Art regularly now on weekends and clearly planned to enter this venerable institution upon graduation. Things were good.

At home, things couldn't have been better. At school there was only one fly in the seemingly sweet ointment of life.

In one's lifetime there are wonderful people who come to you as if they were written as mentors into your personal script. These people you generally remember as the ones who nurtured, reassured, inspired you. Once in a while someone will stand out in your memory as the one person who, by that person's mere existence, impressed and influenced you more than any other. During my high school years, our art teacher, Mrs. Constance Wainwright, was that person. How I hated her.

When I think of it now, it amazes me that through our dislike for Mrs. Wainwright our rat pack of cronies pushed their multiple talents to their limit. We created and starred in plays, wrote poems, and made up entire comic books dedicated to the tedious and loathsome Mrs. W.

Actually, she wasn't such a bad sort. She was just wrong for the job, and not equipped to handle a room full of strong-willed adolescents. By grades eleven and twelve, most of us were serious about our artwork and needed serious instruction. Mrs. W. was a sad disappointment.

Dressed in what we called her "gay summer frocks," Mrs. W. looked as though she'd been standing over a Toronto subway grating. Her wide skirts billowed, the capped sleeves puffed, and her thinning blonde hair flew at right angles to the sides of her head. She spoke with a veddy propah British accent out of the side of her mouth, and the addition of a slight lisp made her wonderfully easy to mimic. Mrs. Wainwright impressions became the rage. Just to stand the way she did and make a characteristic gesture could bring the house down. She became the very catalyst for every bit of satire that came out of North Van High.

Constance Wainwright was a vulnerable woman who meant well. Her easy gullibility was often responsible for her frequent bouts of tears. In breaking her down, we were filled with conflicting senses of both having won and having destroyed something.

It would never have occurred to her, for example, that the paint water we were all drinking was colored with food dye. It would also not occur to her that when half the class excused itself at once, we were all not really going to the bathroom.

When we should have been learning to sculpt with an armature or to paint in oils, we were scribbling on newsprint and making small coil pots out of clay. Angry and frustrated, day by day we plotted against the poor, unwitting Mrs. W.

Behind and to the left of her desk, was the door to the coveted "back room." This seldom opened portal led to the art room mother lode. In the back room were paper and paint and great blocks of clay, and if you could ever get your hands on the stuff, you'd be able to actually *make* something! Although we repeatedly begged for more supplies and larger projects, we were always refused. The back room became a real source of resentment.

"Here," she said, dropping a softball-sized lump of clay on our desks. "Make a pot."

If she hadn't warned us the day before that leaving air bubbles in the clay was dangerous, this particular class would have been much less inspiring. With eye contact and the silent osmosis of communication known only to prisoners of war and malevolent teens, we made a pact. As each small pot was turned in for firing, we wondered what effect all those air bubbles would have on the small back-room kiln.

Apparently, it had happened after hours. None of us really knew for sure, but when school resumed the next day, it was evident that a small explosion had occurred in the art room, and culprits were being sought from within our ranks.

Of the accused, four of us now make our living in the entertainment business (I include myself here), and several others went on to colorful careers in art and advertising. Not one of us was left untouched by the prudish, conservative woman who was our nemesis, and I'm willing to believe that we've all incorporated her character into our artwork in one way or another. It's a shame we lose touch with our high school peers. If given the opportunity to band together once again, I know we'd fondly relive our triumphant demolition of the back-room kiln and remember the bewildered look on the face of Mrs. W. who, still refusing to believe we'd do such a thing, graciously blamed herself.

From my high school annual.

From my high school annual . . . Mrs. Wainwright told me not to clutter my work.

When I began *For Better or For Worse,* I decided that Elly needed a villainous counterpart, someone who would belittle and criticize and create a real tension in the strip. With an inner sense of "getting even" I brought in Connie (after Mrs. Wainwright) and introduced her as a feminist shrew, with few redeeming qualities. After a few weeks, this new character mellowed. She became a rather pathetic single mother. Lonely and confused, she sought solace in her relationships with Elly Patterson, and later, after remarrying, she has become a stable and supportive friend to the rather easily rattled heroine I try so hard to deny is me. When I see how the Connie I introduced has developed into the Connie I draw now, I see that Constance Wainwright has been vindicated. Looking back from the vantage point of my forty-two years, I can admit now that she was a caring and sensitive woman who, pitted against a room full of kids, just never had a chance.

When Connie was first introduced into the strip, she was to be Elly's nemesis . . .

Graduation from high school was something I looked forward to with all my heart. I didn't know that as we said our eager goodbyes, most of us would never see each other again.

I had submitted my folio and been accepted to the Vancouver School of Art. Years of Saturday classes had made the great factory-like building a familiar habitat and I loved being in an atmosphere that was entirely centered around art.

The Vietnam War was raging. Picketers formed small chanting groups at the corner of Granville and Hastings. Signs and posters extolled the virtues of free love. There was a pervasive feeling of spirituality and bonding among the artsies of downtown Vancouver, and we walked in close-knit groups down to the beach or to Stanley Park to do sketches for life class and sculpture.

For someone who once felt that lasting friendship was not

. . . but, within a few weeks, she became an insecure single mom.

within reach, here was a wealth of like-minded comrades who openly expressed their sincere affection.

The Vancouver School of Art was a fine arts college, and during second year, it was evident to me that I was gravitating toward a rather motley little group of commercial illustrators and breaking away from the realists, the impressionists, and the gallery crowd.

My inability to take things seriously had haunted me all through elementary and high school and was again overshadowing my work.

I turned my polar bear sculpture into an aircraft because its nose resembled a Cessna. I glued wire wool into the armpits of my "bust of woman." Perfect renderings of the class skeleton were done of him leaning against a bar smoking cigarettes. My portrait of "a nude, scratching" did not win points.

I moved from the fashionable "in" crowd of abstract expressionists and producers of contemporary art into the realm of the commercial illustrator.

Commercial art, as some saw it, was the bottom of the barrel. Only hacks, people who wanted to do art for a living, went that route, and the school, it seemed, was ill-equipped to train us at the time.

Color was now the norm in magazines. It was rumored that newspapers would be able to reproduce photographs with four-color plates; television had made an immense impact on the advertising industry; and here we were rendering black-and-white tuna casseroles with smudged chalk and friskit paper.

Despite whatever grumbling I may have done, I learned, my work improved, and I had the opportunity to try my skills in a number of mediums.

A doodle from my art-school years . . .

Experimentation was everywhere. The sweet smell of pot often wafted through the courtyard. Fiberglass was new and available and a sudden rush to cast body parts kept the hallways alive with the cries from unsuspecting castees as the plaster they so obligingly allowed themselves to be covered with was removed, tearing the hairs from even their most delicate appendages.

Film workshops were introduced and for one whole season, the entire school was hooked on animation.

Through the generosity of the National Film Board, we were given equipment and professional instruction. It was a tedious and time-consuming effort, but the results were spellbinding. I took home rolls of black leader and tried to emulate the fanciful works of Norman McLaren. I spent hours under the old Bolex camera clicking off drawings one frame at a time. This introduction was all that was needed to convince several of us that here indeed was a field to explore.

In the summer between third and fourth year, I landed a job at Canawest films on Burrard Street. By the time summer was over I knew that I would not be returning to school. This was where I belonged.

The worst part about leaving the School of Art was that I was quitting. I'm not a quitter, and my friends pressured me to reconsider and finish another year. Still, the tiny animation studio had a job for me and was already giving me more to hang onto, more promise of a future than all the courses at the art school put together.

Canawest films was more of a Quonset hut than a building. Hot and sticky in an airless room and pressed shoulder to shoulder were sixteen girls, the cellpainters of the ink and paint department. We were supervised by an ingratiating woman from Los Angeles who had been brought in by Hanna-Barbera to supervise their factory labor.

Scene by scene we colored the Abbott and Costello series. The stories and characters bore little resemblance to the original live productions, and the fruit of our labor was an embarrassing collection of badly animated, mass-produced Saturday morning junk films.

What we did was not as important as how we did it, and I spent coffee breaks and lunch hours in the other departments, learning about backgrounds, storyboards, filming, and the wonderful art of animation.

Although our lives had gone in different directions, I kept in touch with my original high school ratpack of musical and theatrical rowdies, several of whom had entered the high energy world of broadcasting.

It was at a party of would-be media personalities that I met Doug Franks.

Doug was tall and laid-back, he had a deep voice, sleepy blue eyes, and a smile that had mischief written all over it. After a few beers you could always count on him to be the life of the party.

Doug was funny. He was naturally comedic in his gestures and as far as I was concerned, he had all the right qualities in a mate; he was attractive, he liked me, and he could make me laugh.

Doug was working for the CBC as a television cameraman when we were married in 1967. The whole concept of a wedding, to me, seemed a farce: the ceremony, the white, the formality. I infuriated my mother by regarding it as just another party.

For a year, we lived in Vancouver's wonderful hippie west end. I'd lived all my sheltered life in my parents' home and now had my own apartment. I loved the freedom and the title "Mrs."

I continued to work at Canawest, and was learning, bit by bit, to animate. I thought that my career in animation was set in stone (or acetate).

In 1969, the bottom appeared to fall out of the Vancouver broadcasting industry. Spending cutbacks affected every facet of the business. CBC had massive lay-offs, and people were dismissed in order of seniority. Because he was a new recruit, Doug knew that his job was on the line.

We made plans to go east, just for a while, to find temporary work. When the situation improved, we'd go back to Vancouver.

Hamilton, Ontario, is a steel town. Dominated by factories and smelters, the harbor—once a vacationers' paradise—was now an ugly line of warehouses and industrial sites. It was a far cry from postcard-picturesque Vancouver.

As newcomers, not planning to stay, we criticized Hamilton with west-coast arrogance, not knowing how good to us she was going to be.

Doug took a place on the camera crew of CHCH-TV and I, lost without my job at Canawest, searched for something to help pay the rent.

Government employment agencies are at a total loss when faced with an artist. "Yes, but what can you do?" The girl at the Hamilton office asked.

During the day I pounded the pavement; in the evenings, I worked on imaginary assignments to augment my rather unimpressive folio. One of my self-imposed assignments was to do my

. . . and another art-school doodle.

childhood story with a series of "book illustrations." Although I never wrote the book (to be titled "When I Was Lindy"—my nickname for many years), the illustrations were totally consuming. They banished my homesickness for a few hours every day as I recalled, in minute detail, these watercolor scenes of my childhood.

I was about to abandon any hope of resuming an artistic career when an ad in the *Hamilton Spectator* leapt off the page, so to speak.

McMaster University Medical Center needed a graphic artist; someone who could do charts and graphs for medical students— and they wanted someone with audiovisual experience. This I knew I could handle.

I assembled my package of layouts, sketches, and illustrations, added a few pie charts and diagrams just for luck, and nervously set out for an interview.

The address was a nondescript brick building in downtown Hamilton. The room I was sent to was sparsely furnished. The walls were green, the chrome-legged chair he sat on was green, the desktop covering on which I was asked to set my folio was green, and a bilious rush of insecurity gurgled in my stomach as the fiftyish and balding gentleman behind the desk waved me to a seat in the corner.

He had the expressionless stare of a bronze bust; some forgotten political cog, relegated to the darkest corner of an archives building. He was precise, articulate, and imposing. I silently pledged my firstborn to the ministry and prayed, "Please! Please like my work! Please hire me!"

I pulled the matching chair to the side of his desk and stood as I unzipped my beloved leather-like pressed-cardboard art case. Exposing my life's best work, I turned page after page, eagerly explaining a sketch here, a design there, all the while searching his face for a faint glimmer of approval. His eyes, though open and receptive, were focused not on my artistic qualifications but on the miniskirt I wore.

This was the shortest of the short skirts era and the dress I had chosen, though far from improper, was evidently revealing enough. I sat. His eyes sat. I crossed and uncrossed my legs. His eyes crossed and uncrossed.

"Can you draw graphs?" he finally asked.

"Yes," I replied confidently.

"Good. Be at the hospital at nine on Monday."

At a time when Erica Jong, Germaine Greer, and Jane Fonda were all pressuring women to reject male chauvinist porkdom, I rejoiced in the inequality of the sexes, did up my zipper (the one on the art case), and demurely thanked him for his confidence in my ability to draw.

McMaster University was just beginning an innovative program that planned to feature audiovisual technology in its training of medical students. Slide-tape presentations were being prepared and packaged as individual lectures to be absorbed in private booths equipped with small projectors and headsets.

Twenty of the brightest young people (from all points of the globe) were chosen to be the first to take this concentrated course. The programs were designed, they hoped, to make optimum use of everyone's time and energy.

Paul Knowles, jovial, dark-haired, and a little portly, was my supervisor. We were both barely past twenty.

Pioneers ourselves in the new program, Paul and I began to work with the medical teaching staff. We produced, at first, dry, wordy visual lectures, white lettering on blue diazo slides—slide after slide after chart after boring graph.

Several of the doctors, discovering we could actually *draw,* began to give us more challenging illustrations, and one suggested that we both be trained more as medical illustrators than as graphic artists. We were accepted as part of the "team" of young, first year students; we attended lectures, went on rounds, watched and participated in dissections, observed animal experiments, and were treated with great consideration. It was to be the best job I would ever have in my life . . . as nine to five jobs go!

I have always been inquisitive to a fault. "Don't do that because I said so" wasn't good enough. Without a good accompanying reason, I would do whatever I was told not to do and suffer the consequences.

Somewhere within the bowels of every hospital is a morgue. One doesn't have to see this chamber to be aware that it simply exists. A morgue is a matter of fact. To most nonmedical personnel, this room of mysteries was best passed by, quickly and quietly or . . . circumnavigated altogether.

One day, on impulse, I asked if I could watch an autopsy and permission was granted.

The room was a sombre hospital green and smelled of antiseptic, flesh, and formaldehyde. Long shelves supported an assortment of bottles filled with things in cloudy solutions. On a stainless steel table in the center of the room lay the fragile corpse of an old woman. A weigh scale and dissection tools lay on a table next to her. The technicians went about their work, casually discussing their families and the things they did on the weekend.

I watched as the body was opened. All the components, neatly packed one against the other looked exactly like the diagrams in *Gray's Anatomy*.

Each organ was carefully removed, dissected, weighed, and recorded in a notebook.

It occurred to me that this was like one of my father's empty clock cases; the workings out for repairs—or the back of a television set with all the electrical parts removed.

The difference was that no matter how well it was reassembled, no ordinary current could bring life back to this machine.

What magic makes a living, loving, thinking person out of flesh and bone?

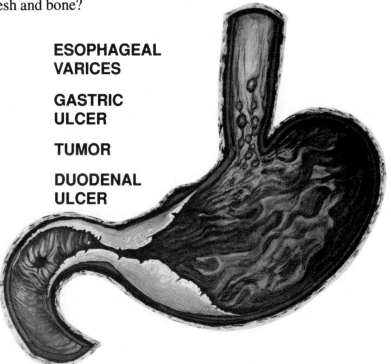

ESOPHAGEAL VARICES

GASTRIC ULCER

TUMOR

DUODENAL ULCER

I loved drawing color illustrations. This was done with animation paint on a number of acetate sheets.

I thought that I had lost all faith in spiritual things when Elly died, but here in this macabre setting, my belief in God suddenly returned. Confronted with the harsh reality of death came the knowledge that there must be a reason for life. There was a spirit!

You learn answers to the most powerful questions in the strangest places!

If work was wonderful, the marriage was not. Friends one day and enemies the next, Doug and I had gone from being Blondie and Dagwood to Flo and Andy Capp.

By now we were too entrenched in the east to return to Vancouver. We bought a small house in Dundas overlooking a pretty ravine. In the evenings, I did freelance work from a greenhouse we turned into a studio. We fought, made up, and fought again.

One day, we went for a drive and came home with an English Sheepdog puppy we called Farley (after the gray and grizzled author, Farley Mowat).

This unruly ball of fuzz gave us something in common, and for a while, we settled into a comfortable domestic routine.

Medical school is a stream of symbols, signs, compounds, diagrams, measurements, and unending facts to be understood and memorized. It was our jobs to make these facts easier to retain. It was the brainchild of one researcher to have us do cartoons to help break the monotony. Having seen some of my less than reverent drawings, David Sackett asked me to work with him on a project. The result was an illustrated survey of wind and water-borne diseases for the Department of Epidemiology and Biostatistics. It was a slide presentation done entirely with cartoons.

Some of the teaching physicians were concerned. It was an affront, some thought, to a time-honored profession to trivialize serious information. Oddly enough, the information conveyed in cartoon form was remembered, where the information on the traditional slides was not.

A new career was born. The serious medical illustration was turned over to the other artists in the department. We now numbered four. A fellow artist and I were given the delightful task of making the sublime ridiculous: a virus attacking a cell became a sword-wielding Oil Can Harry, threatening a damsel in distress; a rat with electrodes implanted in its brain to stimulate sexual interest became a rodential W.C. Fields imagining his rat-shaped rubber cellmate to be Mae West. This was one of those rare times when I couldn't wait to get to work in the morning.

I worked for McMaster for five years, and I understand the teaching staff still uses those illustrated lectures today.

I was twenty-six and wanted a family. My freelance work had increased, and I knew I could establish a small business at home.

The subject of baby drove a wedge between us. Vacillating between wanting and then not wanting a family, Doug finally begged total freedom from the decision altogether. I conceived Aaron.

For the nine months I was expecting him, our turbulent relationship mellowed. I left my job in town and prepared the house and myself for the new baby.

Pregnancy, for me, was not the radiant young woman with the blossoming silhouette one sees in the magazines. It was nausea and swollen feet, old wives' tales, and just plain fear.

Murray Enkin was one of those perpetually good-natured people who put you at ease with a smile. An obstetrician with years of experience and several books to his credit, he was respected and admired by students and patients alike.

I had done many comic drawings for him—mostly about the Lamaze and Leboyer methods of childbirthing. Even though one needed a specific referral, Murray kindly accepted me as his patient.

Every pregnant woman suffers long, annoying waits in the doctor's office. When you are finally admitted to an examining room, you know that it's just the preliminary to another long wait. This time you're a semiclothed captive under a white sheet with nothing to do but stare at the ceiling.

I had been in this position for some time when Murray finally came into the room. "So, where were you—playing golf?" I grumbled. "The least you could do is put some pictures on the ceiling for us to look at!" "You're the cartoonist," he replied with his infectious grin. "I challenge you to do pictures for my ceiling."

During the months that followed, I brought packages of drawings to Murray's office. My thoughts, my impressions, my sarcastic perspectives on pregnancy, I poured out onto my white bond pads in rough, single-panel comics.

The positive response from patients and staff was overwhelming. Murray's encouragement was great. By the time Aaron was born, I had done over eighty cartoons for his ceiling. I wondered why he kept the originals and only put up copies.

New motherhood was not easy. Emotionally, I was still a child myself. Though Doug appeared to be pleased with his small son, he found parenthood too confining and too much of a commitment. When Aaron was six months old, he moved out of the house.

Here I am with Farley—we're expecting Aaron.

No divorce is easy, but I suspect ours was less difficult than most. He left everything that could not be carried on his motorcycle. I was to keep the car, the house—everything—and in exchange, he was to be free forever of all responsibility. This was our agreement.

I had quit my job, my freelance business was generating about $7,000 a year, and I was thrust into a stage of adulthood I had never experienced—complete independence. I wondered could I really depend on . . . me?

With the baby on my back, I peddled my folio from ad agency to ad agency, getting small jobs here and there. I did posters, billboards, television graphics, medical illustrations—I even sent a series of caustic feminist cartoons to *Ms.* magazine. (They were never acknowledged.)

It felt good to joke about divorce and being single. It felt good to joke about feeling ugly and inadequate and unloved. It felt good to joke about the burdens of parenthood. I went back to the old family trait of, "If you can't say it right out—joke about it."

Most of my freelance work was comic art. I was hired by the library and even the local paper to do cartoons on a regular basis. When, after a year of charging ten dollars a cartoon, the *Dundas Valley Journal* dropped my work rather than give me a raise, I realized that I might have to resort to finding a full-time job.

Hoping to enter the market as a book illustrator, I wrote and illustrated a story for Aaron. I took these from publisher to publisher—proof that I could draw, I had an imagination, and could work in color. Some were polite; some were downright rude. None were interested. It amused me, a couple of years ago, to get a call from one of these publishers offering me a job. He even asked if he could produce the little book I'd done for Aaron. I refused. It would be too much trouble, now, to take all those pictures out of their frames (and, besides, the story isn't very good).

I finally landed a full-time job in the layout department of a packaging firm. Welfare covered Aaron's daycare costs—I'll be forever grateful for that.

I was not the best of employees. I hated being at work by 8:30. I found the endless stream of cereal boxes, fertilizer, medicine packages, and sketches of farm machinery a tiresome chore.

I clowned around a lot. If the place (a factory, actually) could not have colorful decor and cheerful surroundings then, by golly, they had *me!* My supervisor put up with a great deal. I was a comic and a nuisance, but he cared for me enough to keep me on.

I have made little mention of Farley the dog. Having discovered that the arrival of a baby meant second-class status, he became increasingly antagonistic toward Aaron, lunging at him in his jolly jumper until he flew in circles. Not realizing that this was inappropriate play, Aaron was thrilled by the ride. Finding it hard to cope with both baby and beast, I eventually gave Farley to a couple who lived on a farm outside of Toronto (his wonderful, bumbling character lives on in the strip).

It was Murray Enkin, my obstetrician, who started me on the path which led to this full-time occupation as a cartoonist.

Aaron was a toddler. I didn't see Murray as often, now, but we kept in touch and he called one day, saying, "I have an idea and I want you to come over to my house to talk about it."

I arrived with kid in tow. His dear wife, Eleanor, opened the door and led us, with a mischievous smile, into the living room. Murray sat on the floor with all eighty cartoons I had drawn for his ceiling, spread around him in order, like a great fan. "Kid," he said, as he popped the cork out of a champagne bottle, "you've got a book."

With the help of mutual friends, Bernard and Marjorie Baskin, and with Murray's persistence and encouragement, I was able to find a publisher. He became my editor. I increased the number to 101 cartoons, and in 1974, my first book, *David, We're Pregnant!* was published.

To my great surprise this irreverent and rather rough little book was something the market seemed to be ready for, and almost immediately it was called a success. With my freelance business doing well, and the prospects of producing books in my future, I impulsively quit my job and began working again at

The cartoons from David, We're Pregnant, Do They Ever Grow Up?, *and* Hi Mom! Hi Dad!, *are reprinted here by permission of Meadowbrook Press. This cartoon is from my first book* David, We're Pregnant!.

Now, if you're carrying low & it shows from the back, then it's a boy---or is that a girl....? Tell me — were you facing North when you conceived?

home. I did a second book *Hi, Mom! Hi, Dad!* and a third called *Do They Ever Grow Up?* These drawings became like a therapeutic outlet, a release for all my worries and shortcomings as a parent. What impressed me most of all was that they seemed to be a welcome therapy for other parents as well.

Cartoons from Hi Mom! Hi Dad!

This cartoon from Do They Ever Grow Up? *shows an early example of a panel style.*

Another selection from Do They Ever
Grow Up?

A selection from Hi, Mom! Hi, Dad!

From Do They Ever Grow Up?

As a freelance graphic artist, and wife of one of the cameramen, I had spent a great deal of time at CHCH-TV, a midsized television station in downtown Hamilton. One of their props people was a rather countryish character who wore black plastic-rimmed glasses, corduroy jackets, and, on occasion, a fur tie which he described as "Rabbit, between seasons." Rod Johnston was from somewhere in Northern Manitoba, and it was rumored he lived in a bread truck parked in a friend's backyard. I never really got to know him, but I instinctively liked him. There was something that attracted me to him . . . a sort of . . . silliness.

What I didn't know was that over the years he'd developed a soft spot for me, and when my marriage dissolved, he hoped to find the courage to call me—sometime.

When you're a single parent, the loneliness is often overwhelming. You're torn between needing your child for the comfort and purpose they provide, and resenting them for their dependency and their very presence in your life. Every social move is restricted when you have a baby.

In *For Better or For Worse,* Connie's single and lonely days were done with the sympathy and understanding that comes from having lived through it myself.

As a divorcee, I rode the rollercoaster of relationships. I had just come to the end of another gut wrenching and empty ride, and on this particular day, when the sky was overcast and the baby was whining in the carseat beside me, I drove to the local airport. Oh to be able to climb into one of those beautiful, tiny planes and fly away from everything!

The sky brightened. I watched a small blue Cessna touch down and taxi toward me. A rather familiar figure emerged and . . . it was the fellow with the fur ties I'd met at CHCH. He ran to meet us and greeted me with such enthusiasm I could hardly speak. (In fact, as Rod tells it he said "Lynn, it's great to see you! How are you?" And I replied "Who the hell are you?")

Well, he invited Aaron and me out for lunch and flew us to the next airport for a hamburger.

Boy, was I impressed! Rod was nice and funny and talented and motivated and he liked me. Here was someone with whom I knew I could be great friends.

On our second "date" I took him to a Polish wedding. We did the polka and told stories and laughed. It was evident that there were possibilities for this relationship. The following Saturday, we sat down at my kitchen table, each of us with a sheet of paper,

The newlyweds—Lynn, Aaron, and Rod

and wrote down all the things we were looking for in a partner. We spared no details. We included such trivia as food and music preferences, we were both adamant that our partner not smoke. Amazingly, our lists matched almost exactly except for one thing. Rod was planning a career as a flying dentist in the Northwest Territories and I wanted to live in the city. If I wanted him I'd have to sell my house in Dundas and move north.

Dentistry was a far cry from the career Rod Johnston had planned. After achieving a degree in broadcasting and spending two years in the business, the glamour had gone. When I met up with him on that windy day in March, he was in his second year of dentistry and his plans were set. He would go back to the North Country he'd grown up in, provide a service to the native communities, and buy a plane—something he'd wanted since childhood.

I could see that life with this man would be more than interesting. It would be an adventure. I agreed to sell the house and go north.

We were married in a small civil ceremony by our friend Rabbi Baskin. Rod resumed dental school and, with his student loans, a small income from the books, and my business, we had enough to support the three of us.

Every day was a pleasure. I had truly married a friend that I loved. I had known for years what it was like to be funny—but to be happy was a new experience.

In the summer of 1977, we were preparing to move to Lynn Lake, Manitoba, a mining town 750 miles northwest of Winnipeg. Rod's folks lived there, and he'd grown up there. We had a waiting family and a good airport. I looked forward to the change and to doing a small book a year on the perils of parenthood.

Rod was in his last month of school and I was expecting Katie. The phone rang, and someone on the other end was asking if I was interested in doing a daily, syndicated comic strip. If I was, would I submit twenty strips right away to Universal Press Syndicate. I was dumbfounded.

My three little books had found their way to the desk of Jim Andrews, who, with the success of Cathy Guisewite's *Cathy,* was looking for a cartoonist to do a strip on family life from a woman's point of view. He wanted something contemporary, a little contro-

Rod and Baby Kate

versial perhaps. Based on the work they had seen, Jim and his associates thought I might be capable.

We were living out of packing boxes. Never one to refuse a challenge, I fired off twenty comic strips to Universal Press Syndicate. I had never developed a set of characters. The only people I knew I could draw over and over again were my family, having doodled cartoons of us on the countless letters I wrote home. The twenty strips featured the Johnston family. We waited for a response from the syndicate, never really expecting to hear from them again.

These are two of the first strips I sent to Universal Press Syndicate in 1978.

Katie had been born by the time we heard from Jim Andrews. With my returned submissions was a critique from the editor, Lee Salem, and a twenty-year contract. I was to look it over and fly to Kansas City as soon as possible.

Sitting across from Jim Andrews, Lee Salem, and John McMeel at the large rosewood table in their boardroom was terrifying. Despite the enthusiasm and confidence radiating from the faces of these articulate, well-dressed people, I was a mess of indecision. I knew I could produce a book a year, but could I be funny, or at least worth reading, every single day? A merciless deadline, I couldn't imagine. What boundless inner resources one would have to possess before agreeing to something like this? I couldn't believe that people would actually *strive* for this job!

Eventually, tired of coddling and reassuring me, they left me alone in the room with the dreaded contract. In the moments that followed, I watched my right hand pick up the pen and draw my signature on the bottom line.

Everyone seemed pleased. There were handshakes and congratulations and someone suggested that we all go out for lunch. I respectfully declined. I went back to my hotel room and was ill.

This is the first daily cartoon strip that was syndicated on September 9, 1979.

We had made the move to Lynn Lake. I worked briefly as Rod's dental assistant while plans and details of my "job" and my contract were being worked out.

Although the contract was signed in 1978, the strip did not appear until September 9, 1979. This year is the tenth anniversary of the strip in print. The other day we added all the Sunday and the daily papers together and the total came to 1,002. I can't believe the time has gone so fast.

Before I could manage a daily feature, I felt I needed the time to create more clearly defined characters. I wanted to practice writing dialogue, learn timing and technique. Lee was a good editor. Here's someone else with a natural affinity for humorous speech and comic writing. With his regular critiques and long phone conversations, I finally felt ready to launch the feature. It was Lee's idea to call it *For Better or For Worse,* as my approach was, in some ways, rather bittersweet. It was Jim Andrews's idea to continue using the real family as the characters. Rod and I felt that using our names would eventually be tiresome, and perhaps embarrassing—especially for the kids.

We decided to change all the names and in the confusion of ideas, simply chose to use everyone's second name. We called the family the "Pattersons." Aaron's second name is Michael, Kate's is Elizabeth and Rod's is John. The only character that did not receive a family name is Elly. I always wanted to remember Elly Jansen in a special, personal way, so I gave her name to the heroine in my strip. This, in a way, is how I've kept her alive. It's also been a way of separating myself from the character who is, so very obviously, me.

For six years *For Better or For Worse* was produced from the

My flying dentist

basement of a yellow house in Lynn Lake, Manitoba. Rod operated a clinic in town and flew our Cessna 185 into the Indian villages for one week of each month. Rod's mother and a kind neighbor took Katie in the mornings. I'd package my strips and walk down to the bus station where the Grey Goose bus would take my work to Winnipeg and the courier to Kansas. In interviews I told southerners that I relied on dog teams—and they believed me. Lynn Lake was a nondescript clutter of frame houses with a few shops on the main street. When we moved there, the population was 3,000. The next town was sixty miles down the road and as small as ours; Thompson was another three hundred miles of dirt road south. We depended heavily on aircraft to get us in and out. We were no

This is Tadoule Lake, one of the native villages where Rod set up his mobile clinic.

strangers to cold weather. The planes rarely flew after minus 40 degrees, and the airport was a focal point for all of us. It meant freedom, it meant company.

Although they rarely mentioned my rather peculiar job, I knew that everyone in Lynn Lake enjoyed the small bit of publicity it brought to Northern Manitoba and now and then the locals couldn't help pointing me out.

Every January the men's curling teams would throw a huge Bonspeil, a sort of drunken showdown, to see which northern team was best. It was customary to hire several strippers and fly them in from Winnipeg for the occasion. One morning following this bawdy event, I sat in the airport lobby with my folio waiting for the Transair flight to Winnipeg. It was horribly cold and windy, the flight was late. The two ladies who had been last night's entertainment huddled in a row of seats chewing gum, groaning from their respective hangovers, and loathing everything about the present situation. The airline representative offered us each a coffee. We were the only passengers there. As he handed a steaming cup to one of the haggard performers he pointed at me. "See her over there?" he said. "Did you know that she does a strip?" Pulling herself up into a sitting position, her pained and painted companion replied, "*Cripes!* Why don't they hire local?" I always considered that a compliment.

Even though I often resented Lynn Lake, this town gave us many lasting friendships. The warmth, the gossip, and the humor all found their way into my work somehow or other. It was a town of colorful relationships. It was a town where "you can steal a man's wife, but you don't touch his woodpile!"

Rod was operating two clinics when the news came that the mine was going to close. He had been the only "flying dentist" in the area and loved the north so much that I think we would have stayed if the town had a future.

In 1984, we left Lynn Lake and moved, with Rod's parents, to a farm just outside North Bay Ontario. It's a pretty spot; far enough north to be home to my beloved bushwhacker and far enough south for me to have a courier and junk food and *malls!* We have a log house and a small black spaniel. Aaron and Kate are sixteen and eleven respectively, three years older than their counterparts in the strip, Rod has a clinic which he built himself and in the summer he rides his bicycle to work. We still own an airplane, but use it only for family outings. Sometimes we yearn for the adventures of the past. All in all, we're an average family.

Like many mothers, I work at home. I have a small studio in the basement and do my most productive work in the morning. For several days a week, I write the text or dialogue—much like one would write a script. (Cathy Guisewite suggested I do this when I called her for advice.)

When I have several weeks written, I draw my panels in pencil. I can draw two to three weeks of panels in an eight-hour day. The next day, I'll ink them in and erase the pencil lines, then I apply a textured film to add some visual interest. I wear animator's gloves while I work because—well, to be truthful, I can't seem to keep from smudging things. I use a flexible, Speedball C-6 nib for all of the actual "drawing"; for straight and ruled lines, I use Rapidographs; #2 nibs for lettering. Pelican Tusche brand india ink for acetate sheets seems to work the best for me. It's very opaque, and doesn't smudge easily. It does, however, clog the Rapidographs which makes for some noisy trips upstairs to the kitchen sink. (One drawback to working at home is that I'm far too close to the refrigerator.)

I like #2 ply, smooth surface Strathmore paper—but, right now, I'm using #3. While visiting Sparky Schulz last Christmas, he mentioned that since he'd changed his daily format from four panels to three, he had a large surplus of old *Peanuts* paper, and didn't know what to do with it. Since his work was exactly twice the size of mine, he sent me all of his old paper. I cut it in half and for the past few months I have been drawing *For Better or For Worse* on the back of *Peanuts*. I've enjoyed the effect this has had on my editors.

My friendships within this business are something I cherish. Cartoonists gravitate toward other cartoonists as do people in self-help groups who all share the same affliction! By reading into each other's work, there's a sense of already knowing that person long before you meet face to face.

Meeting one's heroes is usually just a fantasy. It has been my great fortune to have heroes as friends.

I've taken this opportunity, the tenth anniversary of the publication of *For Better or For Worse* to tell you something about us, something about myself, and how I got started. Perhaps it will encourage other women now working at some back-room drafting table to submit their cartoons to a syndicate. In my experience—anything can happen.

I wanted to answer some of the questions I've been asked, particularly, "Where do the ideas come from?" I write and draw myself and my family, but the insights and personal glimpses are, for the most part, scenes from my childhood. Aaron and Kate, Rod and others, are the innocent models for the characters that play out my fantasies on paper.

Things, indeed, have not changed much since I was a child. Even my brother—the trumpet-playing, easy-going, and quick-witted "Uncle Phil" in the paper—has put up with and understood me for years. To be part of my family is to be part of my work! To know my work, perhaps, is to know me, and over the past ten years this comic strip has helped me to know myself!

Here, then, is my tenth anniversary collection of *For Better or For Worse,* with a liberal sprinkling of some of my favorite Sunday strips as well. I have titled my new black-and-white collection "A Teenager in the House"—for living with a teenager has been yet another traumatic and terrific chapter in the adventure of parenthood.

I have studied comics all my life. I have loved the works of Charles Schulz, Len Norris, Mort Drucker, Virgil Partch, Dik Browne, Mort Walker, and oh, so many more! To be appearing in some of the same publications as *Cathy* and *Herman, B.C.* and *Shoe,* is an accomplishment I never thought possible. I've become part of a unique association of people who wear their hearts on their sleeve, who have a remarkable gift, and who make their living by giving that gift away. If someone had told me thirty-five years ago that I'd be among them, I never would have believed it.

Just before leaving my room, after tucking me into bed, my dad would turn off the light and say, "See you in the funny papers." Somehow, even though I was just a little kid . . . he knew.

The Funny Papers
Ten Years of Color

For Better or For Worse
By Lynn Johnston

ALRIGHT, ALRIGHT, ELIZABETH!... DADDY'S GETTING UP.

I DON'T KNOW... GO GET HER A GLASS OF MILK OR SOMETHING...

For Better or For Worse
By Lynn Johnston

FOR EASTER IS NOT A TIME FOR SADNESS, BUT A TIME FOR REJOICING. JUST AS SPRING AWAKENS SLEEPING FLOWERS AND ANIMALS AFTER A LONG, COLD WINTER, SO EASTER AWAKENS US TO THE WONDERS AND THE LOVE ALL AROUND....

IS CHURCH OPEN EVERY SUNDAY, MOM?

YES, MICHAEL.

THEN HOWCOME WE ONLY COME TWICE A YEAR?

67

For Better or For Worse
By Lynn Johnston

I AM NOT LEAVING THIS HOUSE WITH THIS SAME OLD HAIRSTYLE!

TWIST PIN COMB PIN BRUSH ARRANGE PIN

BRAID PIN TIE POKE JAB COMB

COMB PIN TWIST POKE BRUSH

AAUGH!

OK, OK, I'M READY...

A SMART MAN ASKS NO QUESTIONS....

For Better or For Worse
By Lynn Johnston

FLOOP

ANNIE?... YOU KNOW THAT 24 LOAVES OF BREAD I WAS MAKING FOR YOUR BAZAAR?

FLOUR

WELL... I FORGOT TO PUT IN THE SALT — AND I RUINED THE ENTIRE BATCH!

OF COURSE I HAD TO THROW IT ALL OUT!

... ARE YOU KIDDING? — IF JOHN EVER FOUND OUT, I'D NEVER LIVE IT DOWN!

HONEST, DAD... IT'S BEEN GROWIN' IN THERE SINCE LUNCHTIME!

69

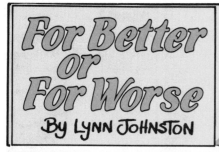

HERE YA GO... COME ON—

TAKE IT... THAT'S RIGHT!

MICHAEL, I HAVE TOLD YOU MANY TIMES NOT TO FEED THE DOG UNDER THE TABLE!

WHAT'S SHE EATING?

BROCCOLI.

BROCCOLI?

HERE, GIRL... NICE LIZZIE...

GRRRR!

SHRIEK

MOM! COME QUICK!— FARLEY'S GOT LIZZIE'S BUNNY!

HE'S SAVED!

MOM WILL FIX HIM, LIZZIE...

—SHE'S SUPER MOM!

... AND MOMENTS AGO I WAS JUST A MILD-MANNERED HOUSEWIFE.

70

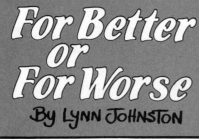

For Better or For Worse
By Lynn Johnston

NIZZIE KISS DOGGIE.

ERK?

NIZZIE SIT ON DOGGIE!

NICE DOGGIE! NIZZIE GIVE HIM PATS.

WHAP! WHAP!

NIZZIE GO FOR RIDE!

NIZZIE PULL EARS!

NIZZIE SIT ON DOGGIE.

WHUMP!!

NIZZIE...

WOOF

FARLEY! BAD, BAD DOG!!

POOR LITTLE ELIZABETH!

HEY... WANNA TALK TO SOMEONE WHO UNDERSTANDS?

For Better or For Worse
By Lynn Johnston

MOM... ELIZABETH JUST WENT OUTSIDE.

MMPHHH

SHE'S GOT HER RED UMBRELLA...

MMMM

AND SHE'S WEARING HER NEW RED BOOTS.

HMZZZz

—AND NOTHING ELSE.

I LIKE SAVING THE BEST FOR LAST.

For Better or For Worse

By Lynn Johnston

HOLY COW! - ANOTHER BATCH OF CHRISTMAS CARDS!

PFLADDAP!

I WANNA SEE! ME SEE!

HMMM .... ALMA, O.K., JESSIE, HELEN BINKS, MARJ AND BERNARD, NANCY AND JIM, FRED AND MAUREEN, CHECK...

WHATCHA DOIN', MOM?

I'M CHECKING OFF PEOPLE WHO SEND ME CARDS.

IF I SEND A CARD - THEN DON'T GET ONE BACK, I CROSS THOSE PEOPLE OFF MY LIST.

"SCRIBBLE" DRAW..

CHRISTMAS CARDS - FOR ME? HOW NICE!

WE WANTED TO STAY ON YOUR LIST.

For Better or For Worse

By Lynn Johnston

BETTER GET OUT OF THE HOUSE IF YOU KNOW WHAT'S GOOD FOR YOU, DAD....

— MOM'S IRONING!

LOOK AT THIS HEAP OF IRONING - AND ALMOST EVERYTHING HERE IS YOURS !!

DON'T GET YOURSELF IN A SNIT..... I'LL IRON MY OWN STUFF!

LARA ♪ TE TAH TE ♪ TAAAH..

HISSSS

A PERFECT JOB!

THAT WAS EVEN ENJOYABLE!

I DON'T UNDERSTAND WHY YOU HATE IRONING SO MUCH, ELLY...

IT'S SO WONDERFULLY MINDLESS !!!

For Better or For Worse
By Lynn Johnston

I HAVE AN IMPORTANT ANNOUNCEMENT TO MAKE....

I WILL BE UNAVAILABLE FOR THE NEXT HOUR....

I AM GOING TO TAKE A **BATH!**

WHO LOST THE PLUG OUT OF THE BATH TUB?!!

I'VE BEEN LOOKING FORWARD TO A BATH ALL DAY — AND NO **PLUG!**

WE DIDN'T TAKE IT!

WHATCHA DOIN', MOM?

POTATOES

LOOKING FOR THE RIGHT-SIZED POTATO!

THUNK!

WHO SAYS A MOTHER'S MIND STAGNATES IN THE KITCHEN !!!

For Better or For Worse
By Lynn Johnston

HARRY'S Hair Shop

OPEN

YACK YACK YACK YACK!

JOHN! WHAT HAVE YOU DONE?!!

I GOT A HAIR-CUT.

BUT... IT'S SO SHORT! — IT LOOKS AWFUL!!

YEAH? — WELL, THE BARBER AND I GOT TO TALKING — AND THE MORE WE TALKED, THE MORE HE CUT!

AAAGH! — I CAN'T STAND IT!! — HOW COULD YOU DO THIS TO — ME?!!

IT'LL GROW BACK. BESIDES — YOU DIDN'T MARRY ME FOR MY LOOKS... YOU MARRIED ME FOR MY GREAT PERSONALITY!!

BRAAK!

....SO MUCH FOR PERSONALITY.

For Better or For Worse
By Lynn Johnston

I DON'T KNOW WHAT'S SO GOOD ABOUT GROWNUP PARTIES....

ALL THEY DO IS TALK.

YACK! YACK!

GOSSIP TALK EAT MUNCH!

HI, THERE! WELL, THANKS, ELIZABETH.

YACK YACK

THAT'S ,UH... INTERESTING STUFF, ELLY — ER, WHAT IS IT?

ELIZABETH!

ECONO SIZE DOG KIBBLE

For Better or For Worse
By Lynn Johnston

OW!

WHAT'D YOU DO, DOC? — BITE YOURSELF?

HEY, DOC! — YOU LOOK A LITTLE DOWN IN THE MOUTH. — ANOTHER HARD DAY AT THE ORIFICE?

HEH, HEH!

I HEAR YOU GOT A LOT OF PULL IN THIS TOWN, DOC! — AIN'T IT THE TOOTH?

HAH HA!

I GOT A SONG FOR YOU — "FILLINGS........ NOTHING MORE THAN...FILLINGS"

HEH HEH HEH

JUST A LITTLE TONGUE IN CHEEK THERE!

HA! HA!

HOPE I DIDN'T NEEDLE YOU TOO MUCH, DOC! — WELL BACK TO THE OL' GRIND!

HA! HA!

JOHN — HOW CAN YOU LAUGH AT THOSE SAME OLD JOKES?

I USE THE SAME OLD LAUGH.

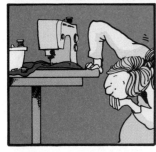

ARE THERE EIGHT ZILLION, KAFILLION, KADILLION, KAJILLION LEAVES IN THE WHOLE WORLD, MOM?

SURE, LIZZIE—WHY NOT?

THE LEAVES SURE ARE PRETTY NOW, HUH, MOM.

I KNOW WHY. DO YOU?

SURE! ALL SPRING AND SUMMER, THE LEAVES MAKE FOOD FOR THE TREE....

UNTIL IT GETS TOO COLD. THEN THE TREE GOES TO SLEEP AND DOESN'T NEED THIS FOOD...SO IT CUTS OFF NOURISHMENT TO THE LEAVES....

AS THE LEAVES DIE, A CHEMICAL CHANGE IN THEM PRODUCES THE COLORS—AND THE COLOR VARIES ACCORDING TO THE SPECIES OF THE TREE!

OH.

GRANDMA SAYS GOD PAINTS THEM.... ONE BY ONE.

CLICK!

BEEE-EEE...EEEEEEE

...EEEEE-EEP! CLICK.... HI, NERD-HEAD! HOOOBADOOBA! WHAT'S UP, DOC? (GIGGLE, SNORT...) BYSIE-WYSIE! ....CLICK ....BEEEE...

EEEP....CLICK...... HAH, HAH, HAH BLAH, BLAH, BLAH BUR-RRP! (GIGGLE, GIGGLE GIGGLE...)

BEEEEEEEEP...CLICK.... ROSES ARE RED, VIOLETS ARE BLUE (GIGGLE...) GORILLAS ARE HAIRY AND SO ARE YOU! (GIGGLE, SNORT, SNUFFLE...

HI, JEAN. ANY MESSAGES ON MY ANSWERING MACHINE?

UH-HUH.

YOUR KIDS CALLED.

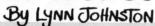

92

For Better or For Worse
By Lynn Johnston

For Better or For Worse
By Lynn Johnston

GOSH, ELIZABETH! ALTOGETHER, YOU GOT 27 VALENTINES!

IS THAT ALL?

MOM, WHY DO THEY ALWAYS SHOW LOVE WITH A HEART? WHY NOT WITH SOMETHING ELSE?

YOU MEAN, LIKE A LIVER OR A SPLEEN?
UH HUH.

WELL, MAYBE IT'S BECAUSE WHEN YOU LOVE SOMEONE YOU FEEL IT... RIGHT HERE.

AND WHEN THAT SOMEONE IS FAR AWAY, THAT FEELING BECOMES SORT OF A DEEP ACHE.

WELL, WHAT WERE YOU AND MOM DISCUSSING SO SERIOUSLY?

SHE WAS TELLING ME ABOUT LOVE.

AND WHAT DOES YOUR MOM SAY ABOUT LOVE?

SHE SAYS IT'S A PAIN.

JOHN, YOU HAVE DONE IT AGAIN!!

YOU TOOK A SHOWER AND YOU DROPPED THE TOWEL ON THE FLOOR!

OH.

I'M ...I'M SORRY, EL.

BELIEVE ME ...I'LL NEVER (SNIFF) DO IT AGAIN!!

PLEASE, PLEASE, PLEASE FORGIVE ME!

BOP!

WHAT'S THE MATTER? CAN'T YOU TAKE AN APOLOGY?

For Better or For Worse
By Lynn Johnston

JUST DRAW A LINE ALL AROUND MY ARMS – THAT'S RIGHT!

NOW WE CUT IT OUT...

OK, LET'S SEE HOW FAR IT WILL WRAP AROUND.

WHAT ON EARTH ARE YOU DOING?

IT'S GRANDMA'S BIRTHDAY, AN' WE DIDN'T KNOW WHAT TO BUY HER...

SO WE'RE SENDIN' HER A HUG!

wrap this around you and hold tight! Happy Birthday, Grandma

For Better or For Worse
By Lynn Johnston

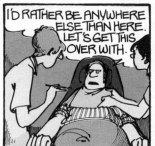

YOU CAN CALL IN THE NEXT PATIENT NOW, JEAN.

HI THERE, RAY! LONG TIME, NO SEE.

SHAPE UP, PATTERSON. YOU KEPT ME WAITING FOR 20 MINUTES.

I'D RATHER BE ANYWHERE ELSE THAN HERE. LET'S GET THIS OVER WITH.

AND I DON'T WANT ANYTHING DONE THAT DOESN'T NEED TO BE DONE! UNDERSTAND?

TAKE IT EASY! AKKK!! WHAT ARE YOU DOING? BLECCH! WHAT IS THAT STUFF?!!

SEE YOU AGAIN IN 6 MONTHS, RAY!

THAT WAS THE MOST IMPOSSIBLE PATIENT WE'VE HAD IN A LONG TIME! WHO IS HE?

MY DENTIST.

For Better or For Worse
By Lynn Johnston

MICHAEL, IT'S POURING WITH RAIN! PUT ON YOUR RUBBER BOOTS.

AW, MOM! NOBODY WEARS RUBBER BOOTS ANY MORE!

HERE. YOU'LL GET SOAKED. TAKE AN UMBRELLA.

I'M NOT TAKING A DUMB UMBRELLA! NOBODY TAKES A DUMB UMBRELLA!!

SLAM!

BUS STOP

For Better or For Worse
By Lynn Johnston

WANNA PLAY ANOTHER GAME, MELODY?

UM... I THINK I HAFTA BE GOING HOME SOON.

I'LL DRIVE YOU HOME, MELODY. ARE YOU SURE YOU KNOW THE WAY?
I'M SURE.

OK, YOU GO DOWN HERE... AN' THEN YOU GO LEFT! NO, I MEAN RIGHT! AND, UH, THEN...

NO, WAIT! YOU GOTTA GO DOWN HERE, I THINK... AN' TURN OVER THERE.

DO YOU RECOGNIZE ANY OF THESE HOUSES AT ALL, MELODY?
UH, NO.

LET'S JUST GO HOME, AND I'LL CALL YOUR MOTHER FROM THERE.

OK, 'CAUSE SHE SAID SHE WAS GONNA COME TO YOUR HOUSE TO PICK ME UP!

WHAT?!!

DON'T WORRY... I GAVE HER DIRECTIONS.

For Better or For Worse
By Lynn Johnston

.MOM!

MOM? UM?

GUESS WHAT! TODAY JULIE HIT HER HEAD ON A SWING, AN' WENT TO THE HOSPITAL!

THERE'S A NEW KID IN OUR CLASS, AN' MARGIE PALMER IS MOVING TO ALBERTA.

WE MIGHT HAVE A SINGER COME TO THE SCHOOL NEXT WEEK. HE TELLS STORIES AN' EVERY-THING!

I JUST ABOUT GOT ALL MY SPELLING TEST RIGHT AN'...

QUIET, HONEY! I'M TRYING TO LISTEN TO THE NEWS!

OH.

...I THOUGHT THAT'S WHAT I WAS TELLING YOU.

For Better or For Worse
By Lynn Johnston

BOUND!

WFV386

ALL RIGHT. YOU CAN COME.

HOLD STILL, FARLEY. THIS WON'T TAKE A MINUTE.

FSSSSSHHTTT

AWK?

YEEEHPE!!!

GET OFF OF ME!

HOWLL!! CUT IT OUT! BARK BARK WOOF!

DON'T! MFF! CALM DOWN! UGH!!!

WHAT HAPPENED TO YOU?

NEVER TAKE THE DOG THROUGH THE CAR WASH.

99

 GOTCHA!!

 YOU'RE DEAD MEAT, MAN!

 HAH! YOU MISSED!!!

 I HATE THOSE THINGS. TOY GUNS ARE AS UGLY AS THE REAL ONES.

 COME ON, EL! SQUIRT GUNS HAVE BEEN PART OF CHILDHOOD SINCE THE INVENTION OF PLASTIC!

THEY'RE A MILLION LAUGHS! THEY'RE FUN! THEY'RE WHAT SUMMER'S ALL ABOUT!

WE'RE NOT TALKING ABOUT A WEAPON, HERE - WE'RE TALKING ABOUT A SIMPLE, HARMLESS...

 SQUIRTT!!

GIVE ME THAT *G☆ GUN!!!

 SHOULD I PUT ON SOME TEA, HONEY?

SURE.

BUT NOT IN THAT POT!!

JOHN, WHEN YOU'RE PUTTING THE PLATES INTO THE DISHWASHER...THEY SHOULD BE TURNED THIS WAY 'ROUND!

WHEN YOU'RE DONE WITH THE DISHES, YOU COULD AT LEAST WIPE OFF THE COUNTER!

-BUT NOT WITH THAT CLOTH!!

YOU WRAPPED THE LEFTOVERS IN SARAN WRAP, HONEY. I ALWAYS PUT THEM IN THESE PLASTIC CONTAINERS.

UH...I THINK I'D BETTER LET YOU DO ALL THIS.

⚡SIGH⚡...YOU KNOW, ANNE, JOHN IS THE SWEETEST MAN ON EARTH...

BUT FOR SOME REASON, HE JUST HATES TO HELP WITH ANYTHING AROUND THE HOUSE!!

I DON'T KNOW WHAT SHE'S READING...... BUT I WANT THAT BOOK WHEN SHE'S THROUGH WITH IT!

MMPH...

YAWNN...... STEP STEP STEP

CLICK STEP

SPLASH!

AAAAUCH! FLUSH

CLICK!

WHACK!

DON'T TELL ME.... I LEFT BOTH SEATS UP AGAIN.

I WANT TO GO INTO THIS HARDWARE STORE, EL... I'LL JUST BE A SECOND.

HIS "SECOND" IN A HARDWARE STORE IS EQUAL TO MY "SECOND" IN A MALL!

HARDWARE and BUILDING SUPPLIES

LET'S SEE... I'LL NEED SOME 1×6, A COUPLE OF 2×4'S, 2 SHEETS OF PLYWOOD, AND 36 FT. OF TRIM.

WE HAVE SOME OF THAT METAL EDGING YOU WANTED JOHN... WHAT IS THE WIDTH OF YOUR HALL DOOR?

GOSH! I DON'T REMEMBER.

JUST A MINUTE.

JUST ADD 4 INCHES ON EACH SIDE.

LOOK AT ALL THE LEAVES, DADDY! THERE MUST BE MILLIONS AN' BILLIONS OF THEM!

DO YOU THINK THAT GOD KNOWS HOW MANY LEAVES THERE ARE IN THE WORLD?

IT SAYS IN THE BIBLE THAT "EVEN THE HAIRS ON THY HEAD ARE NUMBERED."

YOU MEAN THERE ARE ANGELS WITH NOTHING TO DO BUT COUNT LEAVES? SURE. WHY NOT!

WHAT KIND OF JOB WOULD THAT BE?!!

GOVERNMENT.

105

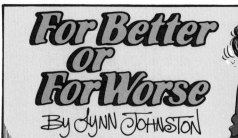

108

 I CAN'T DO THIS! I DON'T WANNA DO THIS! I WON'T DO THIS!!

 THE TROUBLE IS, MICHAEL, YOU'VE LEFT YOUR HOMEWORK 'TILL THE LAST MINUTE!

 YOU'VE LET IT PILE UP AND PILE UP UNTIL YOU'VE GOT AN IMPOSSIBLE AMOUNT TO DO AT ONCE!

 ....IF YOU DID JUST A LITTLE BIT EVERY DAY, THIS WOULD NEVER HAPPEN!

 COULD YOU HELP ME WITH THIS, MOM? NOT NOW.

 HOW COME?

 ....I'VE GOT TO DO THE IRONING.

 WHATSA MATTER, DADDY? I DON'T KNOW, KIDDO.

 ....I DON'T KNOW IF I'M BORED, OR TIRED, OR DEPRESSED.

 EVERYBODY FEELS LIKE THAT SOMETIMES, DADDY. IT'S NOTHING TO WORRY ABOUT!

 WHAT DO YOU THINK YOU ARE - A DOCTOR?

 NOPE - BUT I WROTE YOU A PERSTRIPSHUN!

 THERE! FEEL BETTER NOW?

 IS THAT A NOTE FROM ELIZABETH, HONEY? ... WHAT DOES IT SAY?

 "TAKE TWO HUGS AND CALL ME IN THE MORNING."

111

For Better or For Worse
By Lynn Johnston

OK, EVERYBODY! I'VE GOT SOMETHING VERY EXCITING AND IMPORTANT TO SHOW YOU!

THIS AMAZING LITTLE INVENTION HERE IS A TOILET ROLL HOLDER!

IT IS INSERTED INTO THE CENTER OF THE TOILET ROLL... LIKE THIS!

A SMALL SPRING INSIDE ALLOWS THE ENDS TO BE DEPRESSED SO THAT THIS UNIQUE DEVICE CAN BE PLACED INTO A WALL BRACKET WITHIN EASY REACH OF THE FACILITY!!

NOW! WATCH CLOSELY AS I INSERT THE TOILET ROLL INTO THE TOILET ROLL DISPENSER!!

THERE! WASN'T THAT EASY? DO YOU THINK YOU COULD DO IT BY YOURSELVES? ...WONDERFUL!!!

I CAN NEVER QUITE DECIDE...

—IS SHE IN A GOOD MOOD OR A BAD MOOD WHEN SHE DOES THAT?

For Better or For Worse
By Lynn Johnston

BARK! WOOF!

WOWF! WUFF! BARK BARK BARK!

WUFF? BARK! BARK! WOW-WOW-WOW WUFF!...

WHO LET THE *○ ★⌀ DOG OUT?!!

FARLEY? FARLEY!! FARLEY— COME!

I SAID COME HERE! FARLEY?! COME!! FAAARLEY!

FAAAAARLEY! SNORT? UNH?

WHAT'S GOING ON? I CALLED THE DOG IN.

WHAT FOR?

YOU WANT HIM TO WAKE UP THE ENTIRE NEIGHBORHOOD?!!

IF THAT'S THE LAST POP IN THE FRIDGE, IT'S **MINE**!!

OK, YOU CAN HAVE IT!
SHAKE SHAKE
SHAKE SHAKE

OW! OOH! OW AAAK!!

STOP IT!! WHY CAN'T YOU TWO GET ALONG?!!

LOOK AT YOU. YOU'RE BROTHER AND SISTER. YOU MEAN THE WORLD TO EACH OTHER!

MICHAEL, IF ANYTHING HAPPENED TO LIZZIE, YOU'D BE DEVASTATED!

ELIZABETH, IF ANYTHING HAPPENED TO MICHAEL, YOU'D BE LOST!!

THINK ABOUT HOW SPECIAL YOUR RELATIONSHIP IS AND FIND SOMETHING YOU CAN DO TOGETHER THAT YOU BOTH ENJOY!

OW! UMFF OUCH AAH!

POP!

FTTTTII WHTTTTTT

WHEN I LOOK THROUGH THE YELLOW BALLOON, THE WORLD IS BRIGHT YELLOW!

WHEN I LOOK THROUGH THE RED BALLOON, EVERYTHING IS WARM AN' RED.

NOW ALL I CAN SEE IS BLUE. EVERYTHING'S BLUE. IT MAKES ME SAD.

POP!

THERE! NOW EVERYTHING'S WARM AN' RED AGAIN.

OH, ELIZABETH. I WISH EVERYONE COULD SEE THE WORLD THROUGH BALLOON-COLORED GLASSES!

For Better or For Worse
By Lynn Johnston

YOU CAN'T WEAR THAT CLINIC GOWN, JOHN - IT DOESN'T MATCH YOUR PANTS! IT DOESN'T?

HOW ABOUT THIS ONE? OF COURSE NOT.

HERE. THIS ONE MATCHES YOUR PANTS AND ALSO THE FLOORING IN THE FIRST OPERATORY!

NO! NO! NO! NO! NO! ....I SAID TAN SHOES!

THERE. NOW YOU LOOK LIKE A DENTIST!!

I DO? ABSOLUTELY!

WHY DO I FEEL LIKE AN IDIOT?

For Better or For Worse
By Lynn Johnston

"COUGH" "WHEEZE" "COUGH"

WHONK!!

OOOOH...I HAVEN'T FELT THIS AWFUL FOR AGES!!

I'VE GOT A HEADACHE, MY THROAT'S SORE...I AM NOT GOING TO LIVE.

EMPTY.

MOM! CAN PAUL COME OVER? WE NEED A RIDE TO THE MALL! BY THE WAY, WHAT'S FOR LUNCH?

MOM, COULD YOU PUT MY HAIR IN BRAIDS? CAN WE MAKE COOKIES? HUH?

WHAT MAKES YOU THINK I'M WELL ENOUGH TO DO ALL THIS STUFF?!!

YOU'RE STANDING UP!

 HONEY? MFF?

 I'M GOING TO DROP MIKE OFF AT HOCKEY PRACTICE, AND THEN DRIVE LIZZIE DOWN TO THE SCHOOL. OK? MMMM

THE BUS FOR HER FIELD TRIP LEAVES AT 7, SO I SHOULD GET HER THERE BY 6:45. SNOGGGG...

BYE! SLAM! GZRRKNNNHHHH

 SNORT? SMACK.... SMACK
 YAWNN SCRATCH SCRATCH

 WHERE IS EVERYBODY?!!

 SNORT.

ELIZABETH!! YOU'VE BEEN INTO MY SEWING CHEST AGAIN!!

HOW MANY TIMES HAVE I TOLD YOU TO LEAVE MY THINGS ALONE?!!

AND MY SCISSORS! YOU'VE BEEN CUTTING PAPER WITH MY GOOD SCISSORS!!

ASK FIRST! UNDERSTAND? IF YOU WANT TO USE MY THINGS, I WANT YOU TO ASK FIRST!!!

AS I WAS SAYING.... I'M TIRED OF YOU DOING THINGS BEHIND MY BACK!

A Teenager in the House

A For Better or For Worse® Collection 1988-89
by Lynn Johnston

SUMMER CAMP OH, JEEZ!!

LAWRENCE, BRIAN AND DAWN ARE GOING, SO I THOUGHT IT WOULD BE A GREAT IDEA IF I ENROLLED YOU TWO AS WELL!

"KAMP KAWKAWA"- WOW! THEY GOT CANOES AN' CABINS, MICHAEL! THIS IS GONNA BE GREAT!

WOULD YOU CUT IT OUT! HOW CAN I BE DEPRESSED WHEN YOU KEEP ACTING SO DARNED POSITIVE?!!

SUMMER CAMP! THEY'VE GONE AN' PUT US IN SUMMER CAMP, MAN. WHAT A BUMMER!!

I MEAN, IF IT WAS LIKE THE MOVIES, IT'D BE A BLAST! LIKE, YOU KNOW, "MEATBALLS" AN' STUFF LIKE THAT!

BUT IT'S GONNA BE DULL, MAN! WHY CAN'T LIFE BE LIKE IT IS IN THE MOVIES? WHY IS REAL LIFE SO *G DULL?!!

.... I GUESS IT'S 'CAUSE WE HAFTA BE OUR OWN WRITERS.

COME ON, MIKE! IT'S ONLY FOR A COUPLE OF WEEKS. KAMP KAWKAWA WILL BE A VACATION!

YEAH? LISTEN: "ALL CAMPERS ARE EXPECTED TO MAKE THEIR OWN BEDS, HELP WITH MESS HALL CHORES, BE READY FOR ACTIVITIES ON TIME, AND OBEY CAMP RULES." WHAT KIND OF A VACATION IS THIS?!!

OURS.

WE HAVEN'T BEEN ALONE TOGETHER WITHOUT THE KIDS FOR YEARS, EL! WE'RE GOING TO FEEL LIKE NEWLYWEDS!

WE HAVE THE WHOLE HOUSE TO OURSELVES. I CAN'T BELIEVE HOW MUCH I'M ENJOYING THIS!

ME, TOO.

WHAT'S THE MATTER, EL?

I FEEL GUILTY BECAUSE I CAN'T BELIEVE HOW MUCH I'M ENJOYING THIS!!

THIS IS THE SENIOR BULLETIN BOARD. EVERY DAY YOUR SCHEDULE WILL BE POSTED HERE!

CHECK YOUR TIMES FOR CANOE CRAFT, NATURE HIKES, SPORTS, SWIMMING, RED CROSS, ART INSTRUCTION AND FREE TIME.

NOW, ARE THERE ANY QUESTIONS REGARDING THE ACTIVITIES AT KAMP KAWKAWA?

YEAH!

WHEN DO WE EAT?!

GRAB A TRAY, MIKE! LET'S TRY AN' SIT TOGETHER.

TODAY'S Menu

WOW! GRUB CITY! THEY'VE GOT EVERYTHING HERE!

YEAH!

I WONDER WHY THEY CALL THIS A "MESS HALL."

URP GLFF MMFF GLUT

OH.

OK.... I WANNA KNOW WHO STARTED THE RUMOR THAT KAMP KAWKAWA SERVES ROAD KILL!!

136

ONE MORE DAY ON K.P., PATTERSON, AND YOU'RE A FREE MAN!

GROAN...

EVERYBODY DOES STUFF AROUND HERE! WHY AM I THE ONE WHO ALWAYS GETS IN TROUBLE?!!

WHY AM I THE ONE WHO SUFFERS? WHY ME? WHY, WHY, WHY IS IT ALWAYS **ME**?!

PSSST-HEY, MIKE! WANNA SWIPE ARNIE FELDMAN'S SLEEPING BAG?

YEAH!!!

FEEEWEEETTT!!!

OK, JUNIORS! YOU HAVE AN HOUR OF FREE TIME BEFORE MESS CALL!

GREAT! I'M GONNA LOOK FOR THE PERFECT MARSHMALLOW STICK!

ME, TOO!

YUM'S PUFF MARSHMALLOWS TOAST BEST!

ISN'T IT A BEAUTIFUL NIGHT, ELIZABETH? DON'T YOU WISH YOU HAD A VIDEO CAMERA?

I DO!

I'VE GOT THE ONE IN MY HEAD!!

HOW COME YOU'RE NOT AT THE CAMP-FIRE, MIKE?

I DUNNO.

COME ON. THEY'RE HAVING A GOOD TIME OVER THERE.

NAH. IT'S O.K.

SUIT YOURSELF. WE'LL MISS YOU.

...NOBODY SEEMS TO HAVE MISSED ME YET!

NOBODY LIKES ME. NOBODY REALLY LIKES ME.

SURE, THEY PRETEND TO LIKE ME, BUT WHEN IT COMES TO CHOOSING A FRIEND...NOBODY WANTS TO CHOOSE ME!

THEY ONLY LIKE ME IF I DO SOMETHING DUMB OR ACT SILLY OR TAKE A DARE OR SOMETHING.

WHY DO I HAFTA BE A CLOWN?!! WHY CAN'T I JUST BE BORING AN' ORDINARY LIKE EVERYONE ELSE?!!!

142

WE'RE HOLDING HANDS!...I DIDN'T MEAN TO HOLD HANDS — IT JUST HAPPENED!

I NEVER KNEW YOU COULD SAY SO MUCH WITHOUT SAYING ANYTHING AT ALL.

WHEN I BLOW MY WHISTLE, I WANT YOU ALL TO FIND YOUR BUDDIES AND HOLD UP YOUR HANDS!
FWEEEP!

GOOD! IN SWIMMING SAFETY, YOU ALWAYS SWIM WITH A PARTNER, AND ALWAYS KNOW WHERE YOUR PARTNER IS!!

HEY, LOOK, LIZZIE! YOUR BROTHER'S HOLDING HANDS WITH A PARTNER....

AND THEY'RE NOT EVEN WET!

ONLY ONE DAY LEFT, MARTHA — AN' THEN WE HAFTA GO HOME.
I KNOW.

I, UM...WHAT I WANNA SAY IS...UH...THAT I......

SMACK

WHAT WERE YOU GOING TO SAY?
...I DON'T KNOW. MY LIPS WON'T WORK!!

For Better or For Worse
By Lynn Johnston

You're listening to CKAT Radio 101 on your dial! The sweet sound of country!

STRUMMA STRUMMA STRUMMMMMM

WAL, AH THOUGHT MAH BAYBEE LOVED ME, BUT SHE LOVED MAH MONEY MORE— LEFT 'ER IN MAH 18-WHEELER, AN' AH WON'T GO BACK NO MOOORE...

COUNTRY WESTERN! JEEZ, HOW CAN YOU LISTEN TO THAT CRUD?!

THAT'S THE DUMBEST MUSIC ON THE RADIO, DAD!

HONEST! NOBODY IN THEIR RIGHT MIND LISTENS TO THAT STUFF!

CLICK!

AAHOOOOH, GRUNT, OOOEEEE TWAZANNGGGG OOOEEE, BAYBEE-SPENDIN' ALLA MAH MONEYYY... GONNA BEAT IT, GONNA RETREAT IT! GONNA JUMP INTO MAH PONTIAC, AN' BAYBEE, I AIN'T COMIN' BACK AAHOOOo, GRUNT...

EVER NEAT, MAN! I CAN'T WAIT TO START GOING TO A NEW SCHOOL!

YEAH! JUNIOR HIGH AT LAST—WE'RE FINALLY GETTING AWAY FROM THE LITTLE KIDS.

SOMETHING TELLS ME WE ARE THE LITTLE KIDS!

FIVE TEACHERS, NOT COUNTIN' HEALTH AN' HOMEROOM, MAN... THIS IS GONNA BE INTERESTING!

WE'VE GOT ONE FOR HISTORY ONE FOR ENGLISH, ONE FOR MATH...

YEAH! FOR ALL OF THE ELEMENTARY YEARS WE JUST HAD ONE TEACHER. HOW COME IN JUNIOR HIGH THERE'S SO MANY ?!!

THEY PROBABLY FIGURE THERE'S SAFETY IN NUMBERS!

148

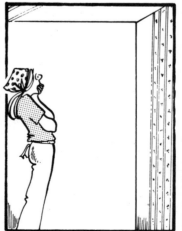

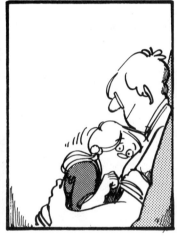

ELIZABETH—WHAT ARE YOU DOING?

SHHH...MICHAEL'S ON THE PHONE.

IT'S RUDE TO LISTEN IN TO OTHER PEOPLE'S CONVERSATIONS, YOUNG LADY!

WAIT A MINUTE. YOU WENT AROUND TELLING EVERYONE I KISSED YOU. YOU KISSED ME, REMEMBER?

JOHN, A GIRL JUST CALLED MICHAEL!

LUCKY GUY!

BUT IT'S A BOYFRIEND-GIRLFRIEND KIND OF CONVERSATION! DON'T YOU THINK HE'S TOO YOUNG?

SHE'S A GIRL, HE'S A BOY. WHAT MAKES YOU THINK IT'S SOME GREAT BIG ROMANCE?

THEY'RE FIGHTING!

WHAT'S WRONG, MIKE?

WELL, THERE'S THIS GIRL. FIRST SHE ACTS LIKE WE'RE FRIENDS, THEN SHE DUMPS ALL OVER ME. AN' NOW SHE WANTS TO BE FRIENDS AGAIN!!

A COUPLE OF DAYS AGO, SHE TREATS ME LIKE A JERK—AN' NOW SHE'S ASKIN' ME TO GO OVER TO HER PLACE AN' HANG AROUND!!

SO, ARE YOU GOING OVER TO HER PLACE?

NAH. I'M GONNA PLAY ROAD HOCKEY.

IF I HAFTA PLAY GAMES WITH SOMEBODY.... I WANT RULES I CAN UNDERSTAND!

For Better or For Worse
By Lynn Johnston

OK, GUYS! I'M CONVINCED. I'M NOT GOING TO MY MEETING TONIGHT. I'M STAYING HOME WITH YOU! HAPPY?

UH HUH.

WELL-SHOULD WE PLAY MONOPOLY? SCRABBLE? DO SOME BAKING TOGETHER? WHAT WOULD YOU LIKE TO DO?

NOTHIN'

NOTHING?!! THEN WHY DID YOU WANT ME TO STAY HOME?

I DUNNO... I GUESS IT'S SORTA LIKE OWNING A DOG.

.... YOU DON'T ALWAYS WANNA DO SOMETHING WITH THEM, BUT IT'S SURE GREAT HAVING THEM AROUND!!

LOOKIT I MADE FOR THE FALL FAIR, DADDY. IT'S A TURNIP! I PUT RADISH EYES, A CARROT NOSE, A PUMPKIN HAT WIF HALFA ORANGE ON IT AN TOOTHPICKS FOR A MOUSTACHE!

I'M CALLING HIM "MR. VEGETABLE HEAD" BY LIZZIE PATTERSON!

THAT'S GREAT, HONEY!

.... IS IT MODELED AFTER ANYONE WE KNOW?

THIS IS AN EMBARRASS-MENT, MOM. EVERYONE IN THE NEIGHBORHOOD GAVE OUT GUM AN' CHIPS, AN' CHOCOLATE!

LOOK AT THIS: LICORICE WHIPS, JELLY BEANS, MILK DUDS, AN ENTIRE BAG OF CARAMEL CORN ....

AND WHAT DO **MY** PARENTS HAND OUT? TOOTHBRUSHES!!

I MEAN, HOW MANY KIDS WANNA GET A TOOTHBRUSH FOR HALLOWEEN?!!

I DON'T KNOW ... AFTER 106, WE LOST COUNT.

YOU SAID TO SAVE SOME OF THIS STUFF FOR ANOTHER DAY .... AN' THIS IS ANOTHER DAY!

MOLLY READY? SURE, DIRK. I'LL CALL HER.

SHE'S STILL GOING WITH HIM? THEY'RE AN "ITEM," EL.

IT'S SERIOUS, I'M AFRAID. THAT GUY IS OVER HERE 'TILL 10:00 EVERY NIGHT! EVERY NIGHT? WHY DO YOU PUT UP WITH IT?!

CHASTITY BEGINS AT HOME.

IT'S BEEN HARD TRYING TO RAISE GREG'S GIRLS, ELLY. THEY TRUST ME, THEY RESPECT ME, BUT THEY STILL RESENT ME 'CAUSE I'M NOT THEIR MOM.

IT'S AS IF I'M TEMPORARY. THEY SEE THEIR MOTHER AS THE PERFECT PARENT. SHE'S THEIR IDEAL!

REALLY? ...WHAT'S SHE LIKE?

I DON'T KNOW. NONE OF US HAS SEEN OR HEARD FROM HER IN TWO YEARS.

176

WE WILL NOW OBSERVE A ONE-MINUTE SILENCE IN HONOR OF THOSE WHO FOUGHT AND DIED IN DEFENSE OF OUR COUNTRY.

WHAT'S THE MATTER, MIKE?

I'VE NEVER SAID "THANKS" TO MY GRANDPA.

LOOK, MOM! THEY'RE RE-PLAYING THE REMEMBRANCE DAY SERVICE! SEE? BY THE CENOTAPH? THAT'S MY CLASS!!

HEY, WOW! A CLOSE-UP! A CLOSE-UP! AWWRIGHT! THAT'S ME!!!

MICHAEL! YOU PUT TWO FINGERS IN YOUR NOSE—AND RIGHT AT THE CAMERA!!

HOW COULD YOU DO THAT ?!!

WHY NOT? IT'S A FREE COUNTRY!

177

178

For Better or For Worse

By Lynn Johnston

JUST GREAT. I COULD BE SPENDIN' THE CHRISTMAS HOLIDAYS WITH MY FRIENDS.

BUT OH, NO! THEY HAFTA DRAG ME ALL THE WAY TO WINNIPEG TO THE STOOPID FARM TO SEE DAD'S RELATIVES!!

WELL, IF THEY THINK I'M GONNA HAVE A GREAT TIME, THEY ARE WRONG. I AM GONNA HAVE A BAD TIME!

CAR RENTAL

I AM GOING TO HAVE A BAD TIME—EVEN IF IT'S FUN.

BEV! DANNY!

HERE IT COMES...

WATCH THE HAIR! DON'T MESS UP THE HAIR!!!

MICHAEL, NOBODY KNOWS YOU OUT HERE! YOU'RE IN ANOTHER PROVINCE, ON A FAMILY FARM MILES FROM ANYWHERE!

I KNOW.

.... BUT AT LEAST I LOOK GOOD.

WELL, IT'S SURE GOOD TO HAVE YOU ALL OUT HERE! MOM AND DAD SHOULD ARRIVE SHORTLY!

THEY'LL HAVE OUR ROOM, YOU HAVE LAURA'S, THE GIRLS ARE IN THE SEWING NOOK AND MICHAEL'S IN THE HALL!

BUT WHERE ARE YOU AND DAN GOING TO SLEEP?

OH, DON'T WORRY 'BOUT US!

IF YOU LIVE ON A FARM LONG ENOUGH, YOU LEARN HOW TO SLEEP STANDING UP!

I DON'T THINK MICHAEL'S ENJOYING THIS, EL.

DON'T BE SILLY.

WELL, IT'S HARD LIVING IN SOMEONE ELSE'S HOUSE. WE'VE HAD PLUMBING PROBLEMS, AND GRANDMA LIKES IT QUIET IN THE MORNING.....

IT'S BEEN FINE! REALLY!

IT'S HARD SLEEPING IN SOMEONE ELSE'S BED, THE KITCHEN'S SMALL, AND...

DON'T WORRY!

STILL, I REALIZE...

WE ARE HAVING A WONDERFUL TIME !!!

OH, BEV, I DIDN'T MEAN TO HURT YOUR FEELINGS!

THAT'S OK.

YOU'VE PUT US UP, YOU'VE DONE EVERYTHING TO MAKE US COMFORTABLE... IT'S JUST THAT, WELL, WE'RE NOT USED TO SO MUCH TOGETHERNESS !!

SO, YOU'LL BE HOME SOON AND BACK TO NORMAL, AND YOU WON'T HAVE TO WORRY ABOUT THIS UNTIL SUMMER TIME!

SUMMER-TIME?

JOHN'S INVITED US ALL TO STAY WITH YOU !!

'BYE! TAKE CARE! SAFE TRIP!

'BYE!

WHAT A CHRISTMAS! I SPENT TWO WHOLE DAYS THAWING PIPES TO A SEPTIC TANK—AND THE REST OF THE TIME FIXING MACHINERY!

THE WEATHER WAS AWFUL, THE KIDS FOUGHT, NOBODY SLEPT.....

WHAT'S THE MATTER, MICHAEL?

SNIFF

WHY ARE THE GOOD TIMES ALWAYS OVER SO SOON ?!!

MOM, YOU STILL SEE COMMUNICATION AS BEING A PAD OF STATIONERY AND A BALLPOINT PEN!

EVERYTHING IS DONE ON COMPUTER NOW. HALF OF MY SCHOOL PROGRAMS ARE ON COMPUTER. THIS IS A NEW AGE!!

GET WITH THE TIMES! NOBODY ACTUALLY WRITES ANY MORE!

....SUDDENLY MY MOTHER AND DAD'S LETTERS MEAN A WHOLE LOT MORE TO ME!

OLD LETTERS

Lynn

I NEVER THOUGHT I'D ACTUALLY FEEL "OLD", CONNIE.

BUT WHEN MY KIDS START TALKING ABOUT COMPUTERS AND THINGS I DON'T UNDERSTAND, IT'S LIKE I'M PART OF A LOST GENERATION!

I KNOW HOW IT IS. JUST WAIT TILL YOU WALK BY A CONSTRUCTION SITE AND EVERYBODY WHISTLES....

...AND YOU KNOW THAT THEY'RE WHISTLING AT YOUR DAUGHTER!

Lynn

EVERYTHING'S CHANGING. I ASKED MIKE TO HAND WRITE A FEW LETTERS AND HE THOUGHT I WAS CRAZY!

WHAT'S WRONG WITH KIDS TODAY? ARE THEY TOTALLY INCAPABLE OF EXPRESSING THEMSELVES WITH THE WRITTEN WORD?

....ALMOST.

NO NUKES

Lynn

WELL, I'D ASK YOU IN, EL, BUT I'VE GOT ANOTHER MEETING TO GO TO.

THE HOSPITAL PROJECT IS DRIVING ME CRAZY. YOU HAVE NO IDEA HOW MUCH WORK THERE IS TO DO!

I DON'T KNOW WHY YOU'RE SO WORRIED, CONNIE. THERE ARE NINE PEOPLE ON YOUR COMMITTEE.

I KNOW.

.... BUT ONLY THREE OF US WORK !!!

OK, GUYS, I HAVE TO BE AT HOCKEY MOMS IN HALF AN HOUR. THERE'RE TV DINNERS IN THE OVEN.

DON'T LOOK AT ME LIKE THAT! IT'S BECAUSE OF YOU I'M GOING! IT'S YOUR TEAM! IF IT WEREN'T FOR YOU, I COULD STAY HOME!!

YOU DON'T HAVE TO GO!

OF COURSE I DO! YOU WANT THEM TO THINK I'M UNSUPPORTIVE?!!

MY MEETING STARTS IN 11 MINUTES. WHY ARE THESE PEOPLE DRIVING SO SLOWLY?!!

YOU ARE DRIVING 3 KM BELOW THE SPEED LIMIT, YOU MORON!! LOOK AT THE TIME!

WHAT ARE YOU DOING? WATCHING THE STUPID SUNSET?!!

SOMETHING TELLS ME I DON'T WATCH ENOUGH SUNSETS.

LET'S FACE IT. THE RINK NEEDS REPAIRING. IT'S GOING TO COST MONEY, AND WE'RE GOING TO HAVE TO FUND-RAISE!

WE SHOULD FORM AN AD HOC COMMITTEE THAT WILL APPLY FOR GRANTS, SEEK SPONSORSHIP, DO PHONINGS AND CONTACT THE MEDIA.

NOW, WHAT WE NEED IS SOMEONE WHO WILL VOLUNTEER...

ERK?

SO, WHAT HAPPENED AT YOUR MEETING, EL?

I'M CHAIRING ANOTHER COMMITTEE.

WHAT NOW?

IT'S AN AD HOC COMMITTEE.

OH. WHAT DOES AD HOC MEAN?

IT'S THE GAGGING SOUND ONE MAKES WHEN ONE FINDS ONE HAS VOLUNTEERED TO CHAIR ANOTHER COMMITTEE!

IT'S NO USE. I CAN'T SLEEP. I KEEP THINKING ABOUT ALL THE THINGS I HAVE TO DO!

WHY DON'T YOU TELL ME WHAT'S ON YOUR MIND. MAYBE IT'LL HELP YOU TO RELAX AND DOZE OFF.

WELL, SHELLEY SAID HARV WOULD FIX THE BOARDS, SO WE CHECKED WITH THE FIGURE SKATERS, BUT THEIR BUDGET WILL ONLY COVER HALF, SO WE CONTACTED THE JUNIOR HOCKEY COACH AND HE SAID THEY COULDN

GZZNORRRKKK

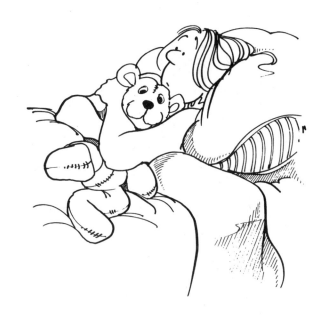

HI, EL... BEEN ON THE PHONE ALL DAY?

203

friendship is very very very very very very very very very very very very very very very very very very very very very very very very very very very very very very very very very very very very very very very very very very very important.

MY TEACHER SAID WE HAD TO WRITE A WHOLE PAGE ON THE IMPORTANCE OF FRIENDSHIP.

AND THAT.... IS A WHOLE PAGE.

WHAT'S WRONG, ELIZABETH?

NOBODY LIKES ME. I DON'T HAVE ANY FRIENDS.

SURE YOU DO! YOU'VE GOT ME AND MOM AND MICHAEL AND FARLEY....

NO, NOT **THAT** KIND!

I MEAN REAL FRIENDS!!

MAYBE NOBODY LIKES ME BECAUSE MY NOSE IS TOO BIG.

WAAAHHH!!

NEVER LOOK IN A MAGNIFYING MIRROR IF YOU THINK YOUR NOSE IS TOO BIG!!

HI, EL, IT'S ANNIE. LOOK, I'VE CALLED EVERYONE AND I CAN'T FIND A BABY SITTER!

MIKE'S ALMOST 13. COULD HE COME OVER FOR A FEW HOURS TONIGHT? I'M DESPERATE!

ICE CUBE! ICE CUBE!

MICHAEL!! DON'T TORMENT YOUR SISTER WHILE I'M ON THE PHONE!!

LIKE I SAID, EL ... I'M DESPERATE.

BABY-SIT CHRIS AN' RICHARD? SURE, I GUESS SO.

HE'D LOVE TO, ANNIE! 7? THAT'S FINE. IF THE BOYS ARE IN THEIR PJ'S, HE SHOULD HAVE NO TROUBLE AT ALL.

THE BABY? OH, I'M SURE HE CAN CHANGE A DIAPER IF HE HAS TO.

BABY?

THEY'RE LEAVING THE BABY?

THERE'S A BOTTLE IN THE FRIDGE FOR THE BABY; HELP YOURSELF TO A SNACK. WE SHOULD BE HOME BY 10.

I KNOW THIS IS YOUR FIRST BABY-SITTING JOB, MICHAEL, SO I'VE TOLD THE BOYS TO BE ON THEIR BEST BEHAVIOR.

CHAAARGE!!!

BLEEP- TAP BLEEDEEP

UM···TWO SOURBALLS, A BOX OF NERDS, A RED LICORICE, THREE JAWBREAKERS, AN' A JELLY HAT.

HAPPINESS IS GETTING TO KEEP THE CHANGE!

WHAM

MOM SENT ME TO THE STORE FOR MILK, AN' I BROKE THE CARTON! AM I EVER GONNA GET IT!

WHEN I GO HOME, SHE'LL KILL ME!!

SNIFF. I HAFTA TELL HER WHAT I DID. I'LL HAFTA TELL HER IT WAS MY FAULT. I'LL HAFTA TELL HER THE TRUTH.

····UNLESS I CAN THINK UP SOMETHING BETTER!

WHO DO YOU LIKE BEST, MOM? ME OR MICHAEL?

I LIKE YOU BOTH.

I MEAN, WHO'S EASIER TO BRING UP? ME OR HIM?

YOU ARE BOTH EQUALLY CHALLENGING.

BUT WHICH ONE OF US IN THIS FAMILY DOES WHAT THEY'RE TOLD THE MOST, IS GOOD THE MOST, AN' IS MOST EASIEST TO LIVE WITH?

.... SHE CHOSE THE DOG.

227

WHO'S COMING FOR SUPPER?

PHIL AND GEORGIA.

AND I WANT YOU TO WATCH YOUR TABLE MANNERS. YOU'RE TO BE ON YOUR BEST BEHAVIOR.

WHY? THEY'RE ONLY RELATIVES.

WE HAVE TO START SOMEWHERE!!

GEORGIA! YOU'VE HAD YOUR HAIR CUT!

IT LOOKS GREAT!

THANKS. I NEEDED A CHANGE.

AT MY AGE, I THOUGHT THE LONG, STRAIGHT HAIR MADE ME SORT OF DOWDY-LOOKING.

YEAH, MOM! WHY DON'T YOU CUT YOUR HAIR? YOU STILL WEAR IT LIKE YOU DID IN THE '60'S WHEN YOU WERE A HIPPIE!

YOUR SISTER WAS A HIPPIE?

SURE! LONG HAIR, PEACE SIGNS, LOVE BEADS, THE WORKS.

WHY DID THEY CALL MOM A HIPPIE?

NEED YOU ASK?

MIKE, I REMEMBER WHEN YOUR MOM TOOK HER GUITAR AROUND TO COFFEEHOUSES AND SANG PEACE SONGS!

YOU DID? YOU ACTUALLY WENT ONSTAGE AND SANG IN FRONT OF PEOPLE?

IT WAS THE '60S, MIKE. EVERYBODY DID!

MOM! HOW COULD YOU EMBARRASS ME LIKE THAT ?!!

DON'T HASSLE ME ABOUT THE '60S, PHIL. WHILE WE WERE MARCHING FOR PEACE, YOU WERE SIPHONING GAS OUT OF DAD'S CAR AND HUSTLING CHICKS AT THE A&W.

WHILE WE WERE SEARCHING FOR INNER TRUTH, YOU WERE PLAYING POOL AND — DRINKING BEER IN JORDAN'S BASEMENT!!

WHILE MY GENERATION WAS TRYING TO UNITE THE WORLD IN LOVE AND BROTHERHOOD—

..... YOURS WAS — BENT ON HAVING A GOOD TIME!!

SIS! ..... IS IT MY FAULT YOU WERE BORN FIRST?

TO THE '60S!

TO THE GOOD OL' DAYS!

TO JOAN BAEZ AND THE BEATLES!

TO LOVE-INS, SIT-INS AND FLOWER POWER!

SO, WHAT DID WE ACCOMPLISH, GUYS? REALLY. WHAT DID THE "LOVE GENERATION" EVER PRODUCE?

US!

MAYBE MICHAEL'S RIGHT. MAYBE I DO LOOK LIKE AN AGED HIPPIE.

I'VE GOT LINES AROUND MY EYES I NEVER NOTICED BEFORE. MY CHEEKS ARE SAGGING. I NEVER NOTICED THAT, EITHER!

THIS IS IT. I'VE REACHED THE POINT WHERE YOUTH GIVES WAY TO THE GRACEFUL LOOK OF MATURITY.

...BUT NOT WITHOUT ONE HECK OF A FIGHT!!

WHAT ARE YOU DOING?

SEEING HOW I'D LOOK WITH A FACE-LIFT.

DO YOU THINK I NEED A FACE-LIFT, JOHN?

OF COURSE NOT.

.... I CAN STILL SEE YOUR NECK.

I'M GOING TO DO IT, CONNIE. I'M GOING TO GET MY HAIR CUT.

I'VE BEEN EXPECTING THAT.

YOU HAVE?

IT'S OUR AGE, EL. YOU THINK YOU SEE THE OL' BOD DETERIOR-ATING, AND YOU RUN OFF IN SEARCH OF A WHOLE NEW IMAGE!

IT'S ALWAYS THE HAIR, EL. WE CUT OUR HAIR. I'VE SEEN IT A MILLION TIMES!

I WONDER WHY.

'CAUSE IT'S EASIER THAN LOSING 10 POUNDS... AND TAKES MUCH LONGER TO GROW BACK!!

IT'S VANITY, FARL. IT'S VANITY THAT MAKES US WANT TO BE WHAT WE'RE NOT.

WHY CAN'T WE BE OBLIVIOUS TO OUR OUTER APPEARANCE? WHY CAN'T WE JUST ENJOY LIVING - LIKE ANIMALS?!

....THEN AGAIN... SOME OF US DO.

I STILL DON'T KNOW ABOUT THIS HAIR, JOHN. DO YOU **REALLY** LIKE IT?

SURE I DO.

YOU REALLY LIKE ME LIKE THIS?

I LOVE YOU.

I LOVE YOU WITH YOUR HAIR CURLY OR STRAIGHT. I LOVE YOU THIN OR CHUNKY - I JUST LOVE YOU, EL. ....LOVE IS BLIND!

....AND KNOWS WHEN TO KEEP ITS MOUTH SHUT.

240

For Better or For Worse
By Lynn Johnston

MICHAEL, THE RUG BEATER IS ONLY FOR CARPETS! THIS ATTACHMENT IS FOR THE FLOOR!

BZRNG BANG! WHZZNNGG GRAK GRAK GRAK BZANG

THE CORD IS GOING TO BREAK! MOVE IT TO ANOTHER PLUG!!

LIZZIE, YOU DON'T NEED THIS MUCH CLEANSER TO CLEAN A SINK!

WHO PUT THE DIRTY LAUNDRY ON TOP OF THE CLEAN PILE?!!

HONEY-YOU ARE CLEANING THE TOILET, NOT PLAYING IN IT!!

I DON'T GET IT, EL...

IF THE KIDS DID ALL THE HOUSEWORK.... HOW COME YOU'RE SO TIRED?

IT'S SO FRESH AND BRIGHT OUT THERE, AND HERE WE ARE WORKING IN A STUFFY HOUSE!

WHY DON'T YOU OPEN THE DOOR, EL, AND LET SOME OF THIS BEAUTIFUL DAY INSIDE!

SOMETHING'S THE MATTER WITH THE DOG, MOM. HE KEEPS LICKING AT A SPOT ON HIS LEG.

IT LOOKS LIKE A DEEP CUT! I WONDER HOW THAT HAPPENED!

GET SOME WARM WATER, SOME ANTISEPTIC AND THE SCISSORS. I'LL HAVE TO CUT AWAY SOME OF HIS FUR.

KNOW WHAT, MOM? YOU'RE THE BEST MOTHER A DOG COULD HAVE.!!

FARLEY'S REALLY LIMPING, MOM, AN' HE'S CHEWED THROUGH THE BANDAGE YOU PUT ON HIM. ...SHOULD WE TAKE HIM TO THE VET?

I DON'T THINK SO. THE WOUND'S NOT INFECTED. ...BUT I WONDER WHY IT WON'T HEAL!

WHAT DO YOU SAY, FARL? SHOULD WE LEAVE IT FOR ANOTHER DAY AND SEE WHAT HAPPENS?

.... SOMETIMES I WISH HE WASN'T SO TRUSTING !!

LICK!

248

SUPPER LOOKS GOOD, MOM. MIND IF I EAT IN FRONT OF THE TV?

THIS WON'T DO YOU ANY GOOD, MICHAEL. I DON'T WANT THAT THING ON FOR TWO WEEKS.

I'M NOT ASKING TO TURN IT ON. I JUST WANNA EAT IN FRONT OF IT.

I'LL COME FOR DESSERT DURING THE COMMERCIAL.

WHERE ARE YOU GOING?

OUT.

I'D LIKE TO KNOW WHERE. WHAT'S THE DIFFERENCE? I CAN'T WATCH TV, SO I MIGHT AS WELL GO SEE WHAT'S HAPPENING. MAYBE GORDON'S PARENTS ARE OUT, AN' WE CAN SWIPE SOME BEER.

YOU ARE STAYING **IN** !!

I AM GOING OUT !!

I AM STAYING IN !

FIND A BOOK, SHE SAYS! HOW'M I S'POSED TO FIND A BOOK WHEN THERE'S NOTHING TO READ AROUND HERE !!?

HMM... DAD'S OLD TEXT-BOOKS.....PHARMACOLOGY, ANATOMY OF THE HEAD AND NECK, HISTORY OF SEXUAL PRACTICES IN NORTH AMERICA...

I FOUND A BOOK TO READ!

NOVEL?

IT IS TO ME !!

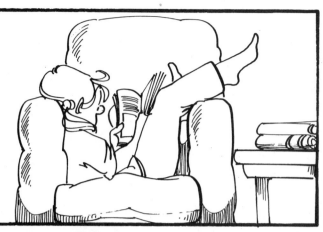

For Better or For Worse

By Lynn Johnston

ELIZABETH, IS THIS YOUR BOOK?

UH HUH.

LOOK AT THIS! YOU'VE FOLDED THE PAGES!

WHEN YOU WANT TO SAVE YOUR PLACE, YOU USE A BOOK MARK!!

OH, DON'T WORRY ABOUT IT.

BUT SHE'S DAMAGING THE BOOKS, JOHN! — HOW CAN YOU SAY "DON'T WORRY ABOUT IT"?!

ELLY.... SHE'S **READING** !!!

A LITTLE TESTY THIS MORNING, ARE WE?!!

MICHAEL, YOU DESERVED THIS PUNISHMENT. NOW ACT LIKE A MAN AND SEE IT THROUGH!

LOOK, IT'S UP TO US TO SEE THAT YOU TWO EMERGE FROM THIS HOUSEHOLD AS WORTHWHILE, RESPONSIBLE — ADULTS! IT'S UP TO US TO GIVE YOU RULES AND GUIDE-LINES!

WHEN WE HAD YOU, WE ACCEPTED A BIG RESPONSIBILITY! MICHAEL, AN IMPORTANT PART OF OUR JOB IS DISCIPLINE!

AND I BET YOU LOVE EVERY MINUTE OF IT.

254